Peer Support in Action

Peer Support in Action

From Bystanding to Standing By

Helen Cowie and Patti Wallace

SAGE Publications
London • Thousand Oaks • New Delhi

SAGE Publications Ltd.
1 Oliver's Yard, 55 City Road
London EC1Y 1SP

SAGE Publications Inc
2455 Teller Road
Thousand Oaks, California 91320

SAGE Publications India Pvt Ltd.
B-42 Panchsheel Enclave
Post Box 4109
New Delhi 100 017

British Library Cataloguing in Publication Data

A catalogue record for this book is
available from the British Library

ISBN: 978-0-7619-6353-0.

Library of Congress catalog record available

Typeset by Keystroke, Jacaranda Lodge, Wolverhampton.

To Corinna (*H.C.*)

For Carol and Jen,
my supporters (*P.W.*)

CONTENTS

TABLES, BOXES, EXERCISES AND FIGURES

Tables

Boxes

Exercises

Figures

INTRODUCTION

The cycle of change

In our experience of working with adults and young people to develop peer support systems in their organizations, we have noticed that the transition to this way of working can be very challenging and even, at times, disturbing. The transition to peer support as a method for alleviating distress in the peer group often involves a major change in the adult's way of relating to young people; it requires, in particular, a shift towards a more democratic, participatory style of teaching and facilitation. Some adults and young people find it challenging, some are inspired, some become discouraged and others are impelled to sabotage the process (Cowie and Olafsson, 2000). It is our belief that those who decide to develop peer support systems will find that the transition is eased by attempting to understand the process of change that is taking place and by working collaboratively over time with the other participants. Developing the stance of reflective evaluation from a range of perspectives is a crucial aspect of this process. We have found it helpful to view the process of transition as a sequence of stages in a Cycle of Change (see Figure 0.1).

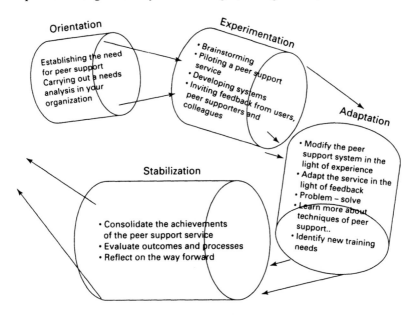

Figure 0.1 *The cycle of change*

In Stage 1, there seems to be a need for some form of *orientation* or preparation for change. The adults in charge of developing the peer support system need to know why they want to develop the new system, what the benefits might be for them and the peer supporters, and what to expect as they make the transition. This is the point at which we recommend that you carry out a needs analysis as described in Chapter 4.

Stage 2 is a period of *experimentation* in which there is a need for sympathetic support from colleagues. The adults and peer supporters at this stage need time and space to brainstorm the problems, to test out new ideas, to pilot. During this stage, they are often anxious about changing and innovating, and vulnerable to sabotage attempts by sceptical colleagues. If progress is not smooth, they may fall back with relief on tried and tested ways. Without the support of colleagues who are tolerant of the dilemmas of change, it is likely that the impetus for innovation will be lost. This is a good time to set up a system for record-keeping, to pilot these systems and to adapt them in the light of feedback from users and supporters. It is also a time to document the process of negotiation and consultation, and to observe the practice of peer support in action, for example during training sessions and supervision. The collection of these forms of data can be an invaluable basis for evaluation. We recommend that you read Chapter 3 for a description of one peer support system in the process of development.

In Stage 3, the time of *adaptation* to the new system of peer support, the survivors of the process are experiencing aspects of the transition that are related to a sense of achievement. New bonds will have been formed within the peer support group. Adults at this stage often report that they experience an urge to find out more about techniques of peer support or to develop their own strategies with confidence. Peer supporters are more confident about their skills and, if their experiences of supervision are good ones, are more skilled at asking challenging questions based on their own experiences of peer support and their observations of its practice. There is still a need for support from colleagues, but their discussion is more likely to be about the craft of working in this way, sharing experiences, problem-solving around difficulties, extending the scope of the system, or even dealing with setbacks in a calm manner. This can be a productive phase where new ideas are tested.

Stage 4 is a time of *stabilization*, when the use of peer support has become a part of normal practice. Adults and peer supporters now enter a period in which ideas are consolidated, when observations on the processes are analysed, when the approach as a whole is refined to guide and improve practice, and when principles are evaluated. This is a good time to look at outcomes, for example reductions in the incidence of bullying, increases in pro-social activity, improved school ethos, reported satisfaction on the part of users and potential users. Chapter 10 will be especially useful at this point.

Practitioners and peer supporters may at this stage choose to stay with the system that they have so carefully built up. Alternatively, they may take the opportunity, created through synthesis and integration, to renew the cycle by defining new aspirations for the system of peer support. This then becomes a stage of orientation revisited, and a means of keeping commitment alive. The stabilization at Stage 4 is in itself a possible foundation for further development, and so a new cycle begins.

The plan of the book

Our focus in this book is on those systems that emphasize emotional support, specifically, befriending, conflict resolution/mediation and counselling-based approaches, and not on those whose emphasis is on education, discussion and mentoring. The book is divided into four parts, each with a different focus.

In Part I, we describe the nature and forms that peer support can take in different contexts, for different purposes and for different age-groups. In this section we describe innovative work on peer mediation by Hilary Stacey and provide a case study of good practice in a secondary school (on a counselling-based intervention) by Paul Naylor. These chapters use original material based on observations of and interviews with peer supporters, their trainers and the teachers in charge of the systems. They give vivid accounts of peer support from the perspectives of those most closely involved in its implementation.

In Part II, we give practical guidance on how to develop a peer support service. In Chapter 4, we offer guidance on how practitioners can undertake an analysis of needs in their own organization. The chapter begins with a discussion of the purpose and uses of the needs analysis, and then the basic elements of a needs analysis are identified and explained. The reader is asked to find and analyse information on the setting and culture of the school/organization, the demographics and other characteristics of the people involved (staff and young people), the problems which the peer support service will be designed to address, the resources available, the desired outcomes and the potential roadblocks. Different ways of collecting the necessary information and their advantages and disadvantages are discussed. Chapter 4 offers information on how to plan an appropriate peer support service based upon the information obtained in the needs analysis, and an experiential exercise is offered to provide practice in doing so.

Chapter 5 covers the major practical issues involved in setting up a peer support service, including selection, management and administration. Under the heading of selection, we describe possible methods of selection of peer supporters as used in a variety of settings, and the advantages and disadvantages of each method. There is discussion of how to manage the selection process in a way that is beneficial to everyone involved: to the young people who are not selected, to those who are, and to the peer support service itself. The section on management describes the type of management which has worked best in peer support services and the resources needed to provide this. In the third section, on administration, we describe key areas that must be addressed in establishing a peer support service. These include: marketing the service; accessing the service; record-keeping; monitoring service uptake and provision; referral; supervision/debriefing; and service review and reporting.

In Part III, we give guidance on how to train young people in peer support. Chapter 6 is about training in the core skills of peer support and covers both the process and the content of training for peer supporters. The chapter begins with process, emphasizing the importance of the trainer modelling throughout the training the behaviour and skills which s/he is asking the peer supporters to learn and use. An enjoyable, experiential style of training is encouraged. Commonly expressed anxieties about these teaching and learning methods are addressed using examples from the authors' and others' experiences. A range of exercises is provided for use in training peer supporters in the core skills.

Chapter 7 focuses on further skills that are needed for young people to learn more complex models of peer support. A selection of exercises and role plays is provided for ongoing practice of basic and more advanced counselling-based skills.

Part IV focuses on ethical issues and the law, the management of supervision, and evaluation of the peer support service that you have established.

In Chapter 8, we focus on legal and ethical issues. This chapter ensures that readers have sufficient knowledge and understanding of relevant legal and ethical issues and their implications to set up and manage a peer support service. Relevant statute and case law, important role, relationship and problem boundaries, and issues pertaining to confidentiality are outlined. Guidelines regarding problems which should not be dealt with by peer supporters are included. There is discussion of the implications of these legal and ethical issues for peer support services, and specific practice guidelines are provided.

In Chapter 9, on debriefing/supervision, the need for adequate debriefing of peer supporters is highlighted. We then offer information on the purposes of debriefing/supervision in peer support, on models of supervision and their relative advantages, and on the skills/behaviours which are useful to someone providing supervision. Common anxieties about providing debriefing/supervision are addressed. On a practical level, we describe some tried and tested formats for debriefing/supervision sessions and an experiential exercise to be used by groups of people who want to practise their debriefing/supervision skills.

Finally, in Chapter 10, we provide guidance on methods for evaluating peer support. In each case, we include an example drawn from a real-life research project. The measures include observations, bubble dialogue, questionnaires, interviews, focus groups and Participant Role Scales. The evaluation methods are presented in a format that we hope will encourage you to develop new measures specific to the kind of peer support system that you have designed.

PART I

WHAT IS PEER SUPPORT?

1

WHY PEER SUPPORT?

They said I was ugly and when a boy asked me out, they said to him,
'Can't you do better than her?' They started to influence his mind, and
when we split up, they were pleased about it and they made fun of me
when I was crying.

(15-year-old girl)

Social and emotional needs of young people

Young people need to have affection, and respectful physical contact with
others; they need to be comforted when they are upset, listened to with
sympathy, taken seriously, and given opportunities to share feelings,
including difficult ones like anger, fear, anxiety and bewilderment. They
need to have access to educational opportunities in contexts that are
supportive, that prepare them for the roles of adult life, and in which there
are resources to help them realize their potential. They also need to gain
the experience of taking responsibility for themselves and others in age-
appropriate ways, and of dealing constructively with the ethical dilemmas
and interpersonal conflicts that they will inevitably encounter in their lives
(Sharp and Cowie, 1998).

Sadly, this does not always happen, and too many young people live in
a state of anxiety or fear, depression or isolation. To make matters worse,
it can seem to the young person that others are indifferent to his or her
distress. This can be compounded by the fact that children and adolescents
often fail to report their unhappiness to anyone. In a nation-wide UK
survey, Smith and Shu (2000) found that the most common response to the
question 'What did you do when someone bullied you?' was 'Ignored

them' (66 per cent), followed by 'Told them to stop' (26 per cent); only 17 per cent 'Asked friends for help'. Girls were more likely to report crying or asking friends for help; older children reported more often that they responded by 'ignoring the bullies'. Over 30 per cent of these victimized young people reported the bullying to no-one and so kept their pain to themselves.

Vulnerable individuals can be especially targeted by aggressive peers while onlookers watch without intervening in support. Craig and Pepler (1995) in a systemic study of peer group relationships found that young people are ambivalent in their attitudes towards the distress of others. On the one hand, they say that they feel sorry for unhappy peers, but, on the other hand, they report that they could join in with others who torment a vulnerable peer. Rigby and Slee (1991) have found that many young people report that they despise weaker or more helpless peers; children and adolescents who are regularly bullied by their peers are more likely to be rated by others as 'someone I do not like'.

Salmivalli and her colleagues (1996) in Finland came to similar conclusions. She identified a number of participant roles in bullying episodes: *victims, bullies, assistants* to the bully, *reinforcers, outsiders* or *defenders* of the victim (see Chapter 10). Assistants join in and actively help the bully to persist in the anti-social behaviour. Reinforcers act as an audience to the bully, laugh at the victim and encourage the bully to do more. Outsiders remain inactive and pretend not to notice what is going on; they can be perceived as colluding with the bullying behaviour though they would describe themselves as neutral. Defenders go to the help of the victim, or comfort him or her after the episode, or go to an adult for help; they may go out of their way to be friends with the victim afterwards and even devise ways of ensuring the victim's safety in the future. However, only around 17 per cent of young people spontaneously act as defenders. Hazler (1996) explains this inaction by arguing that bystanders often do not know what to do and may be embarrassed about sharing in emotionally sensitive experiences. They may also be personally afraid of becoming the object of peers' aggression or derision.

Kochenderfer and Ladd (1997) note that there are gender differences in the strategies that children use in responding to peer aggression. They propose that, since males and females have different peer cultures, the strategies they use may have different effects for boys and girls. They point out that for boys, telling the teacher may be perceived as 'sissy'; it may, therefore, be more acceptable for a boy to fight back or turn to a friend for help. By contrast, girls may not be expected to fight back physically so that telling an adult may be a sufficient strategy to end the victimization. Girls are more inclined to recommend 'socialized tactics' than boys when asked about ways of resolving peer conflicts (Hay et al., 1992). Similarly, Österman et al. (1997) found girls were estimated by peers to use constructive conflict resolution and third-party interventions more often than were boys. They concluded that girls appear to have a greater capacity than boys to analyse and interpret social situations when intervening to smooth over interpersonal difficulties in peer relationships. (Incidentally, Österman et al. stress that girls are not less aggressive than boys but display aggression in a different, usually indirect, way).

As Fry and Fry (1997) argue, socialization and social learning processes play a major part in shaping the behaviour and attitudes of young people. Through socialization within a culture, individuals acquire views on the nature of the social world, develop sets of values and understand the meaning of events within their community. These authors point out that both aggressive and pro-social orientations are strongly influenced by the social contexts in which young people are reared. Aggressive children are more likely to grow up to be aggressive adults; conversely, children who demonstrate pro-social behaviour and attitudes retain this orientation through to adulthood. Parents play a crucial role here. A warm, supportive emotional climate in the home is one that is more likely to produce adults who are co-operative and who adopt a problem-solving attitude towards conflict and distress. By contrast, children who are reared in a cold, frightening emotional climate are more likely to become adults who view the world as hostile and threatening, and who become either defensive and suspicious, or helpless in the face of difficulties.

Within the family, the quality of the child's relationship with siblings has been shown to have an important effect. Older siblings can show great tolerance for younger ones, and can act as role models for the development of social behaviour. They can also show ambivalence and hostility. Dunn and Kendrick (1982), in their observational study of siblings in the family home, noted that the sibling relationship is one in which strong feelings can be aroused – both of love and of envy. But they also documented the powerful feelings of empathy that the sibling relationship can generate. Very early on, children learn from their siblings how to frustrate, placate, tease, annoy, comfort or get their own way. In a follow-up study, Dunn, Brown and Beardsall (1991) found that, by the time of adolescence, someone who had grown up with an unfriendly or hostile sibling was more likely to be depressed or aggressive.

The influence of the community within which young people grow up cannot be underestimated. There are wide variations in the opportunities that societies provide for young people to learn how to act responsibly in relation to one another. All societies appear to have some ambivalence towards young people, treating them as children at times and bemoaning their immaturity at others; it can be difficult to delegate power to young people, or to trust them to act responsibly. In fact, those adults who have tried to mobilize the strength of young people to resolve their own difficulties can meet with hostility or sabotage from other adults and young people too (Cowie, 1998; Naylor and Cowie, 1999). Since some of the issues that cause distress to young people originate in the peer group itself, it is surprising that many adults fail to recognize that the solution may lie with the young people themselves.

Boulton et al. (1999) found that young people who have a reciprocated best friend are much more likely to be protected from aggressive acts or social exclusion on the part of the peer group. The implications of this research are that, in the context of a reciprocated friendship, young people are motivated to help one another against peer relationship difficulties. This confirms the view that vulnerable young people can be protected by appropriate befriending interventions.

The Crick Report (Advisory Group on Citizenship, 1998) has recommended that lessons on citizenship be included in the UK school curriculum. The Government is now committed to the education of 'future citizens' – the young people in schools – with the aim of teaching pupils to be active, responsible members of their school community. The Crick Report stresses that it is important to manage the learning environment in such a way as to encourage pro-social behaviour and to increase co-operative relationships based on trust, among peers and between teachers and pupils. The Report recommends that active citizenship should take place both within the school and in the community:

> It is obvious that all formal preparation for citizenship in adult life can be helped or hindered by the ethos and organisation of a school, whether pupils are given opportunities for exercising responsibilities and initiatives or not; and also whether they are consulted realistically on matters where opinions can prove relevant both to the efficient running of a school and to their general motivation for learning. (Crick Advisory Group on Citizenship, 1998, p. 25)

The Crick Report offers recognition for interventions, such as peer support, that foster co-operative and pro-social behaviour amongst young people.

Furthermore, peer-led interventions highlight the issue of participation in real decision-making. The reluctance of some adults to share power with young people can prevent young people from realizing the interpersonal skills that they actually have and from challenging disturbing facets of peer group social life. Ortega and del Rey (1999), working in Spanish schools, introduced a core curriculum on co-operative learning among peers about democratic principles and practices in everyday life at school. The study of emotions and feelings was involved in three programmes: co-operative group work, life skills and the study of emotions. The three programmes had two central aims: the prevention of violence in schools and education in pro-social values and citizenship. Since 1996, 12 schools in Seville have developed the SAVE project (Sevilla Anti-Violencia Escolar or Seville Anti-Violence Project), modelled on the Sheffield anti-bullying project (Smith and Sharp, 1994), with a high level of satisfaction on the part of the teachers involved. Teachers report that peer collaboration gives them greater awareness of their own emotional interaction with their pupils. One of the outcomes shows that a programme of peer support gives benefits to children who have family and social problems, improves the general climate of the school, and gives social skills training for the peer supporters themselves.

In this book, we maintain that the quality of peer relationships, the roles that young people have in relation to their peers, and the sense of responsibility towards the community that the young person has will affect the young person's sense of self, sense of others and construction of the social world. We argue that peer support systems make a significant contribution to each of the three rights of the child for 'protection from abuse', 'provision of a reasonable quality of life' and 'learning to participate in a democratic society' (CRDU, 1994). In this way, such systems have the potential to contribute to all young people's personal and social education, so enhancing the quality of life in their schools and communities.

What is peer support?

We have reported here on the existence of hostility or indifference on the part of some young people towards vulnerable peers. Fortunately, there are countervailing forces within the peer group itself. Salmivalli (1999) argues that the power of the peer group to promote anti-social behaviour, such as bullying and social exclusion, can be harnessed to end it. She suggests that if young people succeed in addressing the problem, all participants, not only those directly involved, gain a positive experience of active citizenship. She claims that it is possible to 'restructure' networks of aggressive young people and so change the quality of interpersonal relationships for the better. But it is not enough to depend on the spontaneous emergence of helpful support from peers. Young people are much more likely to offer help to their peers in distress if there is a system within which to operate.

How can this be done? As adults, we are in influential positions to create systems which enhance the helpful behaviour that can transform a school or other organization from one that is cold and indifferent to one that is warm, friendly and emotionally open. Peer support builds on the resources that friends spontaneously offer one another, and it can happen anywhere, in any organization, in any age-group. Peer support programmes have been created for young children, adolescents, young adults and senior citizens.

Figure 1.1 gives an overview of those systems of peer support that can provide a framework within which young people can learn how to support one another in times of difficulty.

As Figure 1.1 indicates, peer support takes a number of forms. We have categorized them here into two broad groups: those that emphasize emotional support, including *befriending, mediation/conflict resolution, counselling-based approaches*, and those that emphasize education and information-giving, including *peer tutoring, peer education* and *mentoring*.

Each, in our opinion, has a number of features in common. Peer supporters are usually volunteers, often self-nominated. Members of the peer group often play a part in their selection, and the more the training,

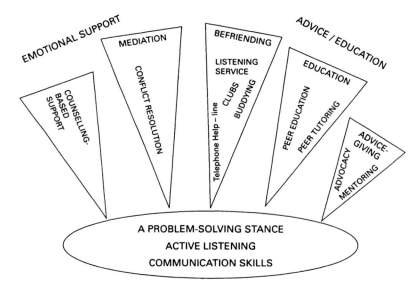

Figure 1.1 *Models of peer support*

the more likely it is that existing peer supporters play an active part in the selection process. Peer volunteers receive need-based, goal-directed and experiential training; they are supervised or debriefed on a regular basis.

Peer support systems require that the peer supporter should be skilled in communication, should be able to listen actively to another person, and should adopt a problem-solving approach to the other's difficulty. Peer support systems, whether formal or informal, tend to incorporate the use of basic listening skills, empathy for a person with social or emotional difficulties, a problem-solving approach to interpersonal difficulties and a willingness to take a supportive role. Adults play a significant role in this process by providing training in a supportive environment. In this way, they give young people the opportunity to offer a direct response to requests for help with regard to a specific problem. They give the peer helpers skills and strategies for enabling users of the system to find solutions to their own problem. Though the immediate work of support is done by the peer helpers, adults retain a supportive and supervisory role without imposing solutions. The non-punitive nature of peer support offers clear and genuine channels of communication amongst those involved.

At what age can children learn to practise peer support methods?

It is highly appropriate, in our view, to introduce peer support methods in the primary school since, by this age, many relationship problems (for example, rejection, isolation, social exclusion and bullying) have become identifiable. Furthermore, there is great diversity among primary school children in the extent to which individuals are accepted and liked by their peers, and the extent to which they feel left out. It is also, according to Aboud (1988), a good age at which to intervene to reduce racial prejudice.

In Table 1.1 we indicate the age-groups for which the various types of intervention are, in our view, most appropriate. As you can see, the most fundamental form of peer support is co-operative group work in the classroom. This can be used at all ages and in all areas of the curriculum. Circle Time, befriending systems and Circles of Friends can be adjusted to meet the developmental needs of young people at all ages. However, we do not recommend that you introduce peer tutoring systems and conflict resolution/mediation earlier than junior school, and again these methods need to be adapted according to the age of the young people involved. Counselling-based approaches, mentoring and peer education methods are, in our view, most appropriate for young people at secondary school and college. In the next section we describe each of these peer support methods in turn with illustrations from a range of age-groups. We recommend that you take a flexible approach in adapting each of the methods to the particular age-group that you work with.

Table 1.1 *The age-groups that can most effectively be trained in different types of peer support*

	7–9 years	9–11 years	11–18+ years
Co-operative group work	Yes	Yes	Yes
Circle Time	Yes	Yes	Yes
Befriending	Yes	Yes	Yes
Circles of Friends	Yes	Yes	Yes
Conflict resolution/Mediation	No	Yes	Yes
Peer tutoring	No	Yes	Yes
Counselling-based interventions	No	No	Yes
Peer education	No	No	Yes
Peer mentoring	No	No	Yes

The peer support methods

We begin with methods that have been successfully used with all age groups – co-operative group work, Circle Time and befriending. Circles of Friends, can also, if appropriately adapted, be used with children from around eight years. Next we describe those that are suitable for children and young people from nine years onwards – Circles of Friends, conflict resolution/mediation and peer tutoring. Finally we describe peer support methods that, because of the issues that they address and because of the complexity of the training involved, are only appropriate for older age-groups in secondary schools, colleges and university – counselling-based approaches, peer education and peer mentoring.

Co-operative group work

We start with co-operative group work, the most fundamental form that peer support can take. This approach is one that all teachers can develop in their individual classrooms to great effect. Galton and Williamson (1992) describe the co-operative primary classroom as one in which children are taught the skills of collaboration through structured activities, including those that help them to deal with conflict. A key characteristic in such classrooms is the time and space set aside for regular debriefing and reflection on the events and interpersonal exchanges that take place in the classroom group. Children are also given the experience of a range of roles within the classroom, such as being a leader, being a recorder of group decisions, being a person who clarifies the goals of the group, being a problem-solver, and being a person who carries out maintenance work like tidying up. Although there can be difficulties in managing disputes and conflicts that inevitably arise in the groups (Cowie et al., 1994), teachers who successfully manage such classrooms are often delighted with the children's capacity to act responsibly and to care for one another. Children also respond with enthusiasm to the challenge of working out rules for their group (Dunne and Bennett, 1990) and regularly evaluating their effectiveness (Foot et al., 1990).

Hanko (1999) offers insightful guidance to teachers on the extent to which emotional and social factors can influence all children's learning and on the ways in which a collaborative approach on the part of adults and children can greatly enhance relationships in the classroom. There is a great deal of evidence to indicate that the experience of co-operation towards peers in the classroom has an influence on children's liking of others and on their friendships. Children who are accustomed to working co-operatively tend to express more positive views of peers than do children who work individually. Research studies suggest that co-operation is a characteristic that can help form friendships and maintain them over time. (For a review of the research in this area, see Cowie et al., 1994.)

What do we mean by this type of peer support? As we have seen, being co-operative means being fair and trustworthy, on the one hand, and having the capacity to address conflict, on the other. Co-operative learning methods can play an important part in children's social and personal development. Co-operative group work provides a setting in which children can explore relationships with one another and can share issues in a trusting environment. When relationship difficulties are being experienced, these methods provide a context in which children can develop a more positive sense of self, effective communication skills and a supportive friendly environment.

As Cowie et al. (1994) argue, there are three essential features of co-operative group work in the classroom:

• Children are prepared to work together outside friendship groups. This type of interaction helps reduce prejudice and fosters trust across gender

and ethnic groups, as well as helping to integrate neglected or rejected children into the peer group.
- Children communicate, share information and divide task-loads in order to achieve a common goal in groups. In the co-operative classroom, the teacher will ensure that there are regular and frequent opportunities for children to engage in tasks that can only be completed by a group effort.
- In co-operative groups, conflicts are discussed and attempts are made to resolve them.

There are many tried and tested methods which teachers can adopt in the co-operative classroom, including trust-building exercises, co-operative games, peer tutoring methods, discussion groups, role play and drama. (For an overview, see Cowie and van der Aalsvoort, 2000.)

Circle Time

We turn now to a particular technique – Circle Time – that has grown out of the co-operative group work approach (Mosley, 1996). This is a method for enhancing effective communication amongst members of a class group, for affirming the strengths of each member of the group, and for creating a safe space in which to explore issues of concern and difficulty experienced by members of that group.

> Circle Time is a time set aside each week when children and their teacher sit in a circle and take part in games and activities designed to increase self-awareness, awareness of others, self-esteem, co-operation, trust and listening skills. . . . As children learn more about themselves and each other, a warm and supportive group atmosphere is built, along with improved relationships. (Bliss and Tetley, 1997, p. 4)

Circle Time usually lasts for about 20–30 minutes, and provides a useful forum for the discussion of important issues, including peer relationships, democratic principles, friendship, justice and individual freedom. The positive atmosphere that is generated in the well-managed circle usually spreads into other areas of class activity. Circle Time gives children the opportunity to:

- discuss matters of personal concern;
- explore relationships with adults and peers;
- develop a sense of being members of a community;
- learn about the experience of reflection and silence.

The emphasis is on positive self-esteem in a climate that is facilitative and non-judgemental. The Circle can become a forum where group members are able to express their needs, negotiate change and mediate in disputes. It is highly relevant to friendship problems and bullying.

The Circle encourages children to think about and reflect on issues. They learn to listen and take turns. They learn empathy for others' feelings, acceptance of others and tolerance on a range of opinions. These aims are encouraged through simple rules (for example, about taking turns and allowing people to speak), a focus on feelings, an emphasis on self-awareness and awareness of others, emphasis on personal responsibility, valuing of each member of the group. The ground rule is that it is the Circle – and not the children themselves – that is tackling the item. There is use of co-operative games to generate an atmosphere of enjoyment and fun.

Circle Time encourages group members to listen to one another, to learn to take turns, to give and receive affirmation, to discuss difficult issues from a problem-solving stance, and to keep to the rules – rules that *they* have played a part in formulating. In one school (Highfield Junior School, 1997) where each class had a regular timetabled period for Circle Time, children used the Circle as a forum for making important rules. One main rule was democratically negotiated by all children through the class circles for the whole school:

Show care and respect for yourself, your friends, your teachers and helpers, your belongings, your school and your family at all times.

During Circle Time at Highfield Junior School, the children also dealt with interpersonal problems in the peer group, including disputes, disagreements and bullying. The members of the Circle had the authority to call on a range of peer-led interventions to help resolve these kinds of problems. They could, for example, call for the support of a 'guardian angel' (potentially any child in the school), a 'house captain' (usually a Year 6 pupil [aged 10–11 years], often with wide experience as a guardian angel, who had been elected by peers) or a 'peer mediator' (a pupil trained in mediation skills). Alternatively, the Circle could refer a difficult issue to the School's Council, a whole school circle that met every two weeks as a decision-making forum.

> Guardian angels came from the idea that you can fly to someone's rescue and guard them. It was a way of taking circle time outside into the playground and having peer support. It meant that someone would be there to support you. A child who is trying to change their behaviour might choose up to three guardian angels to fly into situations which that child can't handle. I'd say that everyone in the school has been a guardian angel at some time. They report on any progress to the class, and the class rewards the guardian angels. (Head teacher, Highfield Junior School, 1997, p. 30)

House captains were elected from Year 6 to offer peer support to younger children in the school. Often, these house captains had been very successful in their roles as guardian angels, as the headteacher explained:

They were doing a grand job as guardian angels, and they were developing ways of doing it. They set up their circles every lunch time to support all the children who were having problems. They were giving advice and using counselling techniques. We realised that they needed training, so that everyone was doing the same thing. We had to adopt ways of resolving conflict fairly and peacefully, without giving ill-informed advice, and without making conflict worse. And the way forward was mediation. (Highfield Junior School, 1997, p. 32)

The children in the school all understood that the peer supporters' brief was to help both bullies and victims, and that mediation was a constructive way forward in changing anti-social behaviour, and in resolving disputes and disagreements. As one pupil, Alan, commented:

Guardian angels are there to help you. They might be your friend or they might be someone else. You can have two or three guardian angels. If you are being bullied they fly to rescue you and help to mediate your problem. If you are trying to improve your behaviour they are around to help you. (Highfield Junior School, 1997, p. 30)

The key to this very successful illustration of peer support in action in a primary school is that, at every stage, the children 'own the problem' and are treated as responsible citizens in their school community. (For a further discussion of the use of mediation in primary schools, see Chapter 2.)

Befriending

Befriending is usually described as an approach that builds on the natural helping skills which children learn through the process of everyday interaction with friends and the family. In some cases this help is purely practical, for example after-school clubs where students offer companionship, activities and refreshments to peers who would otherwise be miserable and alone. Other systems of befriending involve training in active listening, assertiveness and leadership to enable peer helpers to offer support with emotional and social problems, such as being new to a school, having difficulty in making friends, being upset at a separation or loss, being bullied or socially excluded.

Befrienders in secondary schools can be trained to help peers who have suffered traumatic life events. Demetriades (1996) movingly describes the work of the peer partners at Hampstead School, London, in a project known as 'Children of the Storm'. The peer partners offered friendship and comfort to fellow students who had come from war-torn countries, had seen violence and destruction, and were often far from family and friends. They set up an after-school homework/social club where young people could come to study, relax or talk about issues of concern to them. During the years that the project has run, the peer partners have shown creativity in developing new initiatives. For example, in addition to the supportive work at the club, they also give advice and information, brainstorm new ideas, fund-raise, and deliver speeches within school and to outside audiences. As Demetriades (1996, p. 68) writes:

> One thing that has become very clear over the years is that the skills we have acquired by working with war-traumatised children have influenced the way in which we deal with all our students. Our programme of equality works both ways. It has also greatly lifted the status of the peer partners within the school. They are not just older but far more respected.

Circles of Friends

No account of peer support would be complete without mentioning Circles of Friends (Bliss and Tetley, 1997; Newton and Wilson, 1999; Taylor, 1996). Too often, adults advise other young people to ignore a peer who is displaying signs of distress, whether by acting out through aggressive behaviour or by withdrawing into social isolation. By contrast, the Circles of Friends method proposes the opposite stance – one of involvement. The values that underlie the Circles of Friends approach are of 'full inclusion for all; the belief that there is not social justice until each belongs and has an equal place in our schools and communities.' (Newton and Wilson, 1999, p. 5)

The Circles of Friends process provides the opportunity to view from a wider range of perspectives a particular child who is experiencing inter-personal difficulties. Newton and Wilson (1999) identify four concentric circles of relationships, each at a different level of closeness to the person:

- **Circle of intimacy:** The people who are closest to us, often our family. Younger children may include their pets.
- **Circle of friendship:** The people who are our allies and friends. We would confide in them and would expect them to stand up for us when we were in difficulty. Without them we would feel isolated, angry, depressed.
- **Circle of participation:** The people whom we see regularly as colleagues, classmates, in organizations. We see them regularly though they may not be close friends.
- **Circle of exchange:** People who are paid to be in our lives, including doctors, teachers, social workers, therapists. They are paid to give us services or care. There are often professional boundaries (codes of ethics, time pressures, caseloads) that prevent deep personal closeness in this type of relationship.

Newton and Wilson describe the process of setting up a Circle of Friends, with the model of concentric circles as a framework. After prepara-tory work with the focus child and parents there is a meeting with the class.

(This is best facilitated by a professional person, such as a counsellor or an educational psychologist.) The session leader makes it clear that it is unusual to talk about a person when s/he is not present in this way but that the focus child has agreed to the discussion. The leader invites the class to give a picture of the focus child, stressing that only positive things can be said at this point. The next step is to invite the class to list some of the things that they find difficult about the focus child.

There is a general discussion about the role of friendship. The children are then asked to consider their own relationships within the context of the concentric circles model, and, in particular, they are asked to consider how they would feel if the second and third circles were empty – that is, if the only people they had in their lives were family and paid professionals. Children typically respond with words like: 'lonely', 'bored', 'frightened', 'unhappy', 'sad', 'unwanted' and 'depressed'. When the children are asked how they personally would behave if they were experiencing those sorts of feelings, usually they will produce responses like:

- Get into crime.
- Try to get attention.
- Get into drugs.
- Run away.
- Go and hide.
- Steal people's things.

This is a turning-point since the children have demonstrated that they know what a person would do if s/he was isolated or socially excluded. When they are asked what could be done to help, typically they produce two clear solutions:

- Offer the focus child friendship.
- Find ways to keep the child on track with his or her behaviour.

Next the facilitator invites the class to list the things that might make it difficult for the focus child to change.

It is against this background of honest responsiveness that the Circle of Friends can be formed. The group facilitator then enlists the help of volunteers who will form the Circle of Friends for the focus child, usually between six and eight children.

This procedure, with appropriate adjustments for the particular individual, is effective for focus children who show aggressive or isolated behaviour, who are about to start as a new member of the class after, for example, having been excluded from their previous school, or who have been experiencing learning difficulties.

When the Circle of Friends meets, it is important for each member to affirm the positive characteristics of the focus child before going on to the areas of difficulty. Graphics and flow charts can also be used to record the problem-solving process. The facilitator must ensure that the Circle is not threatening to the focus child. The next task is to work out strategies for supporting the focus child in making changes to his or her behaviour. In order to establish the unique identity of this particular Circle of Friends, the group is given a name agreed by all members, and the times of the series of regular (usually weekly) meetings are noted.

Experienced facilitators comment frequently on the depth and richness of the support offered by Circle members. Children are also ingenious in devising practical strategies for defusing potentially difficult situations involving the target child. This is a creative and innovative approach for using the resource of peer support to offer help to troubled and troubling children and to form a peer network for individuals who experience difficulties in their relationships and behaviour.

Conflict resolution/mediation

Conflict resolution and mediation approaches offer a structured method for empowering young people themselves to defuse interpersonal disagreements among peers, including bullying, racist name-calling, fighting and quarrelling. These methods are reported to result in a substantial decrease in the incidence of aggressive behaviour (Konfliktrådet, 1999; Nersnæs, 1999; Stacey and Robinson, 1997). Trained peer mediators meet as a team to encourage problem-solving between individuals who are in disagreement. The method is 'no-blame' and the aim is that each disputant comes away from the mediation with a positive 'win-win' experience and the sense that the outcome is fair to both sides. Mediation and conflict resolution build on listening skills by adding a step-by-step process that facilitates individuals who are in conflict to agree to a mutually acceptable solution. The main components include the idea that conflict is not bad in itself; that conflict need not be a contest; and that it is important to distinguish between what people want and why they want it. Nersnæs (1999) describes the use of mediation programmes of intervention in Norwegian schools. During the mediation, the pupils themselves are responsible for resolving the conflict and for working out a joint solution. Through participation in the process of mediation, pupils develop competence in handling conflict, gain insights into its origins and its solution and acquire new communication skills. (For a more detailed account of peer mediation, see Chapter 2.)

Peer tutoring

Peer tutoring is an educational strategy for facilitating skill gains that has a long history for enhancing school achievement (Topping, 1988; Topping and Ehly, 1998). It is characterized by specific role-taking since at any point one person is in the role of tutor and the other in the role of learner. Its focus is on the curriculum and the peer tutor is usually provided with structured materials to enhance the learning of the tutee. It is particularly successful in helping students with special learning difficulties, for example in reading and mathematics. Topping (1998) identifies three types of peer tutoring in literacy – paired reading, cued spelling and paired writing. Paired reading is suitable for cross-ability tutoring, whether same- or cross-age; cued spelling and paired writing can be used for both fixed-role cross-ability tutoring and reciprocal-role same-ability tutoring. What they have in common is that they 'scaffold' the learning process through the interactive nature of the tutoring and they encourage the learner to be more successful in managing his or her own learning. The outcome is often the development of greater awareness of learning processes.

Reviews of the literature on peer tutoring have consistently found that there are positive cognitive and social benefits for at least some of the participants, and no study has shown that there are detrimental effects. Foot and Howe (1998) point out that this does not mean that peer tutoring is superior to adult tutoring. Rather, it affirms the benefit of face-to-face interaction and dialogue with a sympathetic, supportive tutor, and the value of guided participation in a structured learning activity. One exciting finding in the research is that even children with learning difficulties can benefit in the role of tutor as well as learner.

Topping and Ehly (1998) review the research literature on peer tutoring and conclude that there are clear gains for the learners. (For example, in one study synthesizing the results of over 1,000 pairings, it was found that the average paired reader gained 4.2 months in reading age for accuracy and 5.4 months for comprehension). There are also gains for the tutors in terms of consolidating their own learning and gaining additional social skills. Furthermore, the gains do not wear away, and teachers note that the motivation and confidence of the learners has increased. Peer tutoring has also been successfully applied to subject areas of the curriculum, such as mathematics and science.

Counselling-based interventions

Counselling-based methods extend the befriending and mediation approaches into interventions that are based more overtly on a counselling model. Training is often carried out by a qualified counsellor or psychologist. Peer supporters are given a wider repertoire of counselling skills, and supervision is modelled on professional counselling supervision, usually facilitated by someone with knowledge of experiential work. This approach is generally implemented through a formal system of referral soon after the request for help has occurred, and can include telephone help-lines, individual meetings or small group sessions. Cartwright (1996) trained secondary school students to act as co-counsellors to peers in distress. Using the principles of co-counselling, students:

learn how to re-discover their natural ability to give and get good attention from one another through basic listening skills. These skills are then used on a structured basis whereby, through mutual consent, people of all ages and backgrounds assist one another in co-counselling sessions to 'discharge' (emotions) confidentially and free themselves from the damaging effects of old hurts. (Cartwright, 1996, p. 101)

The outcomes were encouraging since, over time, the school became a safer place to be, and there was a noticeable change in the emotional climate. Younger pupils in particular stated that, even if they never used the service, they felt secure knowing that a peer supporter was there to help them should they get into some difficulty. (For a more detailed account of a counselling-based system in action, see Chapter 3.)

Peer education

Peer education is defined by Finn (1981, p. 91) as 'the sharing of information, attitudes or behaviors by people who are not professionally trained educators but whose goal is to educate'. At a time when budgets are tight and demand for information is high, peer education offers a low-cost opportunity to meet the growing need for information on sensitive topics. But it offers more than an economical solution. Peer education usually involves the sharing of ideas and resources about sensitive life issues by individuals who have 'credibility' within the peer group, and who are perceived to have understanding of, and empathy for, the concerns of that group. Their style of presenting information is likely to be informal and tolerant. Because there is a more balanced educator/participant relationship, it is likely that there will be more open discussion about important concerns.

Peer educators are usually close in age to those with whom they work, although some programmes involve older students working with younger ones. They are often actively recruited to reflect a balance of age, gender and ethnicity. Through training, they become highly aware of the importance of recognizing the impact that factors such as ethnicity can have on people's capacity to understand key issues, for example around sexual behaviour and health. Often they work informally to help the peer group share areas of concern, overcome misconceptions and address ignorance or prejudice about the topic. The focus is usually on health education to facilitate the exchange of information about such topics as smoking, drugs, drinking and driving, gang membership, sexual behaviour and sexual harassment. The peer educators are trained to provide an accurate, factual, non-judgemental and up-to-date resource (Mathie and Ford, 1998).

Zielasko et al. (1995) describe the in-depth programme of training undertaken by peer educators in the university sector. The peer educators are given a great deal of information on content areas, including drugs, alcohol, diversity issues, sexual behaviour, safer sex, eating patterns and eating disorders. In addition, they are trained to feel comfortable in discussing sensitive issues, give presentations that are critiqued by their trainers and peers, and have regular supervision to update knowledge and resolve ongoing difficulties in practice.

Peer mentoring

Peer mentoring is being increasingly adopted in organizations as a means of enhancing efficiency and workplace relationships. There is a great deal of anecdotal support for its use, though not much rigorous research. In companies, it covers the whole spectrum from induction of new staff to training at senior management level. It has been introduced to schools, colleges and universities as a means of enhancing students' motivation and opening up their horizons. Mentoring is also widely used in initial teacher education, and the concept of peer mentoring is now in common use in secondary schools in the UK.

Peer mentoring involves a supportive one-to-one relationship between a younger student (the mentee) and a more experienced student (the mentor). The mentor acts as a role model and aims to promote heightened aspirations, to offer positive reinforcement and open-ended support, and to provide an arena in which to develop a problem-solving stance to important life-span development issues, such as career choice. Mentoring is often, though not always, targeted at disadvantaged groups. Mentors will sometimes work between schools and, through their training, will mentor students in schools other than their own. Mentors can play an active part in projects such as work experience.

Frisz (1999) trained peer advisers/mentors to work effectively with clients from multi-ethnic backgrounds in the USA. They collaborated with professional counsellors to help young people deal with such diverse issues as adjustment to college, personal difficulties and careers guidance. Because the mentors were perceived as being 'on the same wavelength' as users of the service, they were approached by a wide spectrum of the student body. Frisz concludes that through this kind of peer support young people who might never approach an adult counsellor can be greatly helped through the process of discovering their own goals and values.

Sarris (1995) describes a peer mentoring system in which specially trained students on a university campus act in the role of resident staff who live in halls of residence and, under the weekly supervision of trained counsellors, take responsibility for the well-being of fellow student residents on their 'floor' or 'area'. Their role is to refer students to counselling when appropriate, to foster a sense of community and to maintain conditions conducive to academic and personal development. They are expected to spend sufficient time in the building to be perceived as a leader in the hall of residence community. Participation by minority students in this study has been high, with around 35 per cent of the positions being held by such students. Training is extensive and ongoing, and covers such issues as money (including student loans), mental health and stress management, suicide prevention, leadership, eating disorders, domestic violence, alcohol problems and information on sexually transmitted diseases.

Evaluations indicate that the scheme is highly successful. The role of resident staff member is also a highly rewarding one that enhances personal development, increases social skills and develops a greater sense of responsibility.

2

MEDIATION AND PEER MEDIATION

Hilary Stacey

This chapter will begin by defining what mediation is, and in particular how it differs from other forms of conflict resolution such as negotiation and arbitration. It will give a brief history of the development of mediation as a process for resolving disputes, both in schools and in society at large, before moving on to review the research to date into the effectiveness of peer mediation in schools. At a time when schools are increasingly turning to mediation as a strategy to reduce conflict between peers, it is perhaps more important than ever to clarify exactly what mediation is (and isn't), where it has come from, and what it can offer.

A definition of mediation

The process of mediation that is commonly used in peer mediation schemes in schools is the same as the process that is used in mediation in the community. Technically, mediation is a structured process in which a neutral third party assists voluntary participants to resolve their dispute (Cohen, 1995; Stacey, 1996a). Mediators do not set out to decide right or wrong, apportion blame, or even focus on the past any more than is necessary to help the disputants to work out a way forward for the future. Mediators do not offer solutions, and their only control over the process is their insistence that the disputants adhere to the ground rules. These are that each must allow the other to speak without interruption, speak about the other with respect, and talk about the problem from their own point of view without blaming or accusing. Mediation allows the disputants to define the problem from his or her own point of view, identify and express their feelings and needs, hear the feelings and needs of the other person, acknowledge each other's point of view, create solutions, agree a course of action, and evaluate progress at the end if necessary. Haynes (1993, p. 3), writing about family mediation, has defined it as follows:

Mediation is a process in which a third person helps the parties in a dispute to resolve it. The outcome of a successful mediation is an agreement that is satisfactory to all the disputants. The agreement addresses the problem with a mutually acceptable solution and is structured in a way that helps to maintain the relationships of the people involved.

It is common for people writing about mediation (Acland, 1990; Cohen, 1995; Stacey, 1996a; Save the Children/West Yorkshire Probation Service, 1993) to compare it with more traditional or widespread methods of conflict resolution in order to clarify its particular qualities. Cohen (1995, p. 28) represents the difference between negotiation, mediation and arbitration diagrammatically as shown in Figure 2.1. This figure shows the increasing role and control of the third party. Whilst Cohen makes it clear that all three methods of conflict resolution are part of a continuum and equally valid, he goes on to say: 'Proceeding from negotiation to mediation to arbitration, the process becomes increasingly formal and disempowering to the parties.' Mediation, then, unlike negotiation, requires a third party, and, unlike arbitration, requires an equal balance of power between the mediator and the disputants.

Both Cohen (1995) and Acland (1990) compare mediation with arbitration. Acland sees it as more effective than arbitration because it is flexible (it can be formal or informal depending on the circumstances), voluntary (it offers the disputants a risk-free means of finding out more about the other disputant's position), cost-effective, fast, and finds common-sense creative solutions. He also feels that mediation builds relationships through aiming for 'win–win' solutions.

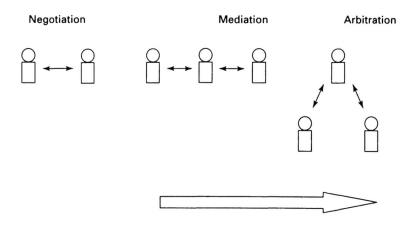

Increasing control of third party

Figure 2.1   *Cohen's comparison of negotiation, mediation and arbitration*

Cohen (1995) compares the two, as shown in Table 2.1. Stacey (1996b, p. 3) has represented the sharing of power in mediation and arbitration as shown in Figure 2.2.

Table 2.1 *Cohen's comparison of the main elements of mediation and arbitration*

	Mediation	Arbitration
Distribution of power	Disputants retain power over the process and outcome.	Arbitrator retains power over the process and outcome.
Impartiality	Mediators guard against taking sides.	Arbitrators may aspire to impartiality, but often have obligations to the system in which they work.
Third-party judgements	Mediators remain non-judgemental throughout the process.	Arbitrators' primary function is to formulate a sound judgement about the disputants' situation.
Disciplinary function	Non-punitive.	Punitive. Arbitrators often have power to enforce punishment.
Temporal orientation	Future-orientated.	Focus on past actions, and blame.
Winners and losers	'Win–win' solutions based on negotiation and compromise.	Solutions imposed by arbitrator may make one or both disputants feel like losers.
Voluntariness	Voluntary participation in process.	Participation often mandatory.
Definition of the dispute	Dispute defined by the disputants, underlying issues teased out and explored.	Arbitrators define the dispute in accordance with rules they are expected to uphold.
Confidentiality	Disputants informed in advance of limits to confidentiality.	Confidentiality often not raised as an issue.

The main difference between mediation and arbitration as processes for dealing with disputes is that in mediation two disputants attack the problems that they share rather than each other. In Figure 2.2 the arrows representing the focus of the attack show that the mediator is able to support the disputants to attack the problem rather than each other by not taking sides. This involves a certain level of social and emotional maturity for the disputants (Goleman, 1996) and the role of the mediator is central to ensuring that the process will not break down.

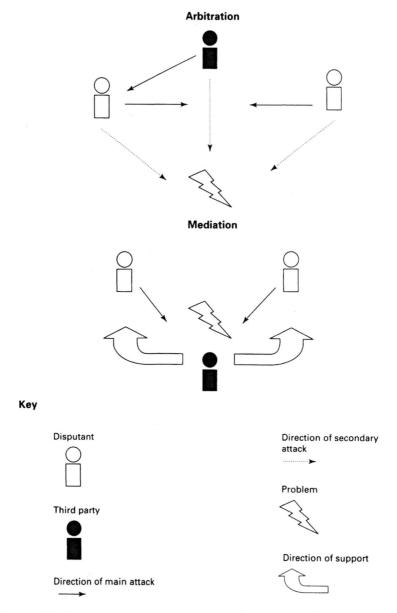

Figure 2.2 *Stacey's comparison of power-sharing in mediation and arbitration*

Save the Children/West Yorkshire Probation Service (STC/WYBS, 1993) compare the 'old retributive' and the 'new restorative' paradigms of justice in their victim–offender mediation handbook. The differences between retributive justice and restorative justice are similar to the differences between mediation and arbitration quoted above. In particular, they stress that under the traditional system of retributive justice, crime is defined as a violation of the state: it focuses on establishing blame and guilt, and uses adversarial methods to impose pain and punishment to deter and prevent future crime. Both the victim and the offender remain passive, with the victim and his/her community largely ignored. Under retributive justice there is no encouragement for repentance and forgiveness and offender accountability is defined as taking an abstract punishment that is unconnected to the original crime. Under restorative justice, they suggest that crime is defined as a violation of one person by another and justice is defined as conciliation based on outcomes that are agreeable to both parties.

Dialogue and negotiation enable the victim and offender to identify offender liabilities and obligations and to identify a means of restitution. A victim's rights and needs are central to the process, and there is scope for repentance and forgiveness which can remove both the stigma and the hurt of the original crime. Again, participating in this process requires a certain level of social and emotional maturity from victims and offenders, and the general support and skills of the mediator are necessary to ensure safety and trust.

It will be evident from the above that arbitration is used by many teachers as a first response in a conflict situation. Traditionally, schools have taken their guidance for conflict resolution from models structured hierarchically such as those involved in the retributive legal system (Polan, 1989). Arbitration may sometimes be the most appropriate response, but if over-used it will deny young people the opportunity of learning to resolve their own disputes effectively. Schools intending to use peer mediation as a method of dispute resolution may well need to review attitudes towards power, justice and punishment.

Mediation has its roots in humanistic psychology, which developed out of the writing of individuals such as Rogers (1951) and Maslow (1962). Both mediation and humanism have their philosophical roots in phenomenology, which grew out of the existentialism of the 1940s and 1950s (for example, Sartre, 1948). Phenomenologists value the recognition of the subjectivity of experience over the quest for objective truth, accepting that there are differing possible interpretations of the same events. Humanistic therapists, teachers and mediators use a phenomenological approach in conflict situations which does not attempt to discover 'right' answers or impose fixed moral rules.

A history of mediation as a process for resolving disputes

Mediation is relatively new in the United Kingdom, both in schools and in the wider community (in 1997, Mediation UK, the umbrella organization for community mediation schemes, had 110 member organizations, with 25 school mediation services). The philosophy of non-violence which underpins mediation has much older roots, however. These can be traced to many world religions, especially eastern faiths. In the United Kingdom, many of the school mediation services that are members of Mediation UK are funded and supported by the Religious Society of Friends (Quakers), which has long experience of using mediation in its work.

The process of mediation that is currently used in the United Kingdom in schools and community projects came from the United States in the 1980s. In the 1970s, the administration of President Jimmy Carter encouraged the creation of the first Neighborhood Justice Centers. The goal of these centres, often known as 'community mediation programmes', was to provide an alternative to court proceedings where citizens could meet to resolve their disputes. Some of the most active of these centres were in New York, Los Angeles and Philadelphia. In the typical community mediation programme, a cross-section of neighbourhood volunteers were trained to mediate the disputes that arose in their community, including disputes between neighbours, family members, tenants and landlords/landladies, consumers and salespeople, friends and small businesses. Some disputes were referred directly to the centre by local residents; others came through an affiliation with local courthouses and social service agencies. The success of these early programmes was impressive (Cohen, 1995). They thrived in a post-1960s climate that demanded non-violent, localized responses to conflict. Exponents in the field (see, for example Beer et al., 1987) were often motivated by strong personal convictions, and sought to enskill and empower citizens to resolve their own disputes in a way that would strengthen communities, and enable individuals to live more satisfying lives.

In the 1980s and early 1990s American lawyers and businesspeople coined the term Alternative Dispute Resolution or ADR (Acland 1990; Adler, 1987) to describe the growing number of non-adversarial approaches to conflict and alternatives to litigation that were being used in the business community. The field of conflict resolution, which had its origin in the 1960s and 1970s with the work of writers such as Boulding (1962), Deutsch (1973) and Druckman (1977), also became a growing area of study in its own right in both the United States and other parts of the world (Burton, 1990; Fisher and Ury, 1981; Sandole and Sandole, 1987). The Institute for Conflict Analysis and Resolution at George Mason University in America continued to support research in this field, and the Centre for the Study of 'Conflictology' was established in Moscow in 1990. Community mediation as a concept also spread to other countries in the 1980s.

Acland (1997) outlines six current areas of mediation in the United Kingdom: community, family, commercial, organizational, environmental and international/political. The area of community mediation, which includes victim–offender mediation, continues to grow. The Criminal Justice Act in 1991 recommended that magistrates consider wider use of community and combined probation disposals rather than using custodial disposals. There is a growing interest amongst sociologists in victim–offender mediation (Cook, 1995; Davis et al., 1992; de Haan, 1990). The use of family mediation is also set to rise sharply over the next few years in accordance with the Family Law Act (1996). There is a growing interest in this area of mediation amongst both sociologists and the general public (Haynes, 1993; Kelly, 1990; Maresca, 1995; Severson and Bankston, 1995). Alternative Dispute Resolution is now a multi-million dollar business in America, and the School of Law in the University of Missouri–Columbia publishes the *Missouri Journal of Alternative Dispute Resolution*, which is dedicated to this field. There are currently a number of British companies offering a commercial mediation service (the Centre for Dispute Resolution, CEDR, in London, for example, which lists a number of large companies as its clients and mediation is increasingly being used as a management strategy (Ross, 1996). Young people currently in UK schools will almost certainly have more exposure to mediation in their adult lives than has hitherto been the case. Peer mediation initiatives in schools will have an increasing role to play in preparing young people for changing attitudes towards conflict in the future.

A history of peer mediation

In the 1980s, in the United States, a range of social, political and pedagogical influences combined to create ideal conditions for the growth of peer mediation (Cohen, 1995). Social problems were causing numerous problems for schools. Despite the educators' best efforts, student conflicts and violence were increasing, and as a result schools were more willing than usual to look outside the educational establishment for assistance. Peer mediation was seen as an additional tool that did nothing to detract from existing structures of conflict management in school. It was seen as a practicable and measurable process (in contrast to peace education, which was seen as vague and politically charged) and it had the added advantage of being visible and media-friendly. Peer education programmes generally had captured the interest of educators (Johnson and Johnson, 1980), and the growth in community and business mediation programmes mentioned above led to an increased understanding amongst the general public. In 1984, a small group of community mediators and educators formed the National Association for Mediation in Education. At that time, only a handful of peer mediation programmes existed. Currently there are many thousands located in schools in every state of the United States.

Throughout the late 1980s and the 1990s the use of peer mediation spread to other parts of the world. Its use is widespread in Canada, Australia and New Zealand (Cameron and Dupuis, 1991; McMahon, 1997), and educational practices which involve peer mediation are growing more common in Europe (ENCORE, 1997). In the UK, the Kingston Friends Workshop Group was amongst the first to adapt American peer mediation training materials for British pupils (KFWG, 1988). In 1989, Walker's paper on violence and conflict resolution in schools, commissioned by the European

Union, included documentation about peer mediation and led to the formation of the European Network of Conflict Resolution in Education (ENCORE), which is supported by British Quakers and continues to meet annually for a conference. There has been a particular interest in conflict resolution training and peer mediation in Northern Ireland as part of the Education for Mutual Understanding (EMU) curriculum (Tyrrell and Farrell, 1995).

In the early 1990s, the climate in UK schools was receptive to peer mediation, as the climate in American schools had been ten years earlier. There were other initiatives in education at that time based on a similar humanist value-system. A greater emphasis on group-work, co-operative games and problem-solving (for example, Bennett and Dunne, 1992; Horbury and Pears, 1994; Leimdorfer, 1990; Masheder, 1986) aimed to improve young people's ability to co-operate. Classroom practice encouraging individualized and autonomous learning tried to give young people a more internal locus of control (Brandes and Ginnis, 1990; Maines and Robinson, 1994; Roberts, 1994; Waterhouse, 1983). A focus on speaking and listening skills (Barnes, 1984; Bliss and Tetley, 1997; National Curriculum Council, 1989; Powell and Makin, 1994) aimed to improve pupils' ability to communicate, and a growing awareness of the importance of high self-esteem (Maines and Robinson, 1988; White, 1991) meant that many teachers were working to establish positive 'affirming' relationships with young people. Other links can be found with initiatives involving schools councils, democratic schooling (Acton, 1989; Andrews, 1989), anti-bullying drives, peer tutoring and peer counselling (Cowie and Rudduck, 1988; Cowie and Sharp, 1996; McNamara, 1996; Topping, 1996; Webb and Kaye, 1996), education for citizenship (White, 1989), world studies (Bobbett, 1996; Nutall, 1990) and Circle Time (see Chapter 1). Above all, what these initiatives stress is the importance of pupil empowerment. Some schools which had begun the process of empowering pupils to take more responsibility for the quality of life in school found that peer mediation was a natural next step to take.

Peer mediation in practice

Stacey and Robinson (1997) provide some guidelines for setting up peer mediation services in schools based on their experience of establishing such services in the UK, mainly in the Birmingham Local Education Authority between 1991 and 1999. They stress that peer mediation services must be integrated into school life, suggesting that they need to be more than a 'bolt-on' feature. They add that they should be included in the school development plan, and written into school policies on behaviour management, anti-bullying and pastoral care. In the schools where they feel the services have been most successful, the staff, including the lunchtime supervisors, have had at least one in-service training session after school dedicated to peer mediation, and ideally a full training day. They give an example of this when the pupil mediators from Alston Junior and Infants School came in on a training day and taught the whole staff mediation skills. Farley-Lucas et al. (1996) also suggest a holistic approach is needed as it values perspectives on conflict from across the whole school community, but particularly from pupils.

In the services that Stacey and Robinson have supported, the 'peer' in peer mediation can refer either to a small number of pupils within a year-group trained to offer a service to others of the same age, or to older pupils mediating younger pupils throughout the school. It can also refer to a team made up of pupils drawn from across the year-groups. Pupils will normally have covered foundation work in conflict resolution and have had an introduction to the mediation process before they nominate themselves or others for further training, which takes place off-timetable over three days. An intensive period of time such as this allows for team-building, proper rehearsal of counselling skills and for the pupils to develop their own guidelines for effective practice. Included in this training are the members of staff who will support the peer mediators throughout the year, lunchtime supervisors, and any other adults or ancillary staff offering their support (education social workers, school nurse, secretarial staff, parents, governors, home/school liaison workers, etc.). Although peer mediators have ownership of their service and make decisions about the way in which the service runs, they also have regular adult support and supervision. This support varies according to the age of the pupils involved, but all have a weekly team-meeting to debrief, to share experiences, and to keep up a regular programme of review and development.

When the services are initially set up, decisions are made about what sorts of problems are appropriate for pupil mediators to deal with, and how pupils access the service. The finer details of rota and responsibilities for running the scheme from day to day are also considered (see, for example, Haigh, 1994). In many models, the service takes place at lunchtime four times a week. Some choose to withdraw into a quiet room or private corner, whilst other services operate out in play areas at a designated spot (see, for example, Brace, 1995, who describes how the pupils at Highfield Junior and Infants School in Birmingham mediate under a tree in the playground). Stacey et al. (1997) found that peer mediation services are more likely to be well used when a high profile is maintained throughout the school year. In many of these successful initiatives, teams of mediators gave themselves a clear identity, choosing names (Trouble Busters, Helping Hands and Untanglers), logos, slogans ('Release the peace and be strong') and forms of identification such as baseball caps, badges and sweatshirts.

The usual stage at which pupils are trained to become peer mediators is at top junior level or secondary level. Stacey and Robinson (1997) do, however, give one example of top infant children (7-year-olds) being trained to mediate successfully for their peers in a rudimentary way.

Uniquely, Stacey and Robinson differentiate between an infant, junior and secondary mediation process. In this differentiated process, infants mediate in the sense that they can support two people in disagreement to hear each other's feelings and agree what to do for the best. Juniors, however, are able to provide a neutral, non-judgemental service in which they can help disputants to understand what the problem is about, appreciate each other's point of view, and choose a way forward. Secondary pupils use their growing maturity, perception and sophistication to reach underlying issues as well as to identify unexpressed needs. A mediation between primary pupils may be over in a matter of minutes. Older pupils may need recourse to several sessions of mediation before reaching a resolution to their dispute.

Research into the effectiveness of peer mediation

Research into the effectiveness of peer mediation programmes tends to be descriptive and informal, and most of it has been carried out in the United States. Where programmes have been evaluated, the responses are consistently positive. Gentry and Benenson (1993) found that 27 grade 4 to 6 (ages 9–11 years) 'conflict managers' experienced a decline in the frequency and intensity of conflicts with siblings as a result of peer mediation training at school, and that parents perceived a similar decline in the frequency of such conflicts and in their need to intervene. Crary (1992) evaluated the effects of a peer mediation programme conducted in a large, culturally diverse, urban middle school. He found that all of the 125 disputants who used the service and managed to resolve their conflicts were satisfied with the outcomes. Teachers also indicated that the amount of conflict in school was lowered. Miller (1993) describes a Maryland middle school that initiated a peer mediation programme in response to increasing numbers of fights. She found that after one year both the number of suspensions given by teachers, and pupil arguments observed in school, decreased. School climate and the quality of pupil relationships improved, and many pupils used the mediation process both within and outside of school. Thompson (1996) and Rogers (1996) also report positive results for the use of a peer mediation programme. Stuart (1991) is one of the few researchers into peer mediation to use quantitative data analysis. She used interviews and questionnaires to evaluate a 'Conflict Manager' programme developed for third- to fifth-grade (ages 8–10 years) pupils in an elementary school in Virginia. The results showed that the programme reduced tension, enhanced pupil self-esteem, increased pupil levels of responsibility, increased the teaching time for staff, and improved pupils' problem-solving, communication, co-operation and critical thinking skills.

Johnson and Johnson (1994, 1996) review a number of evaluations of, and studies on, peer mediation. The overall findings of their research in 1994 show that between 85–95 per cent of disputes mediated by peers resulted in lasting and stable agreements. Pupils trained in mediation engaged in less anti-social and more pro-social behaviour in school. Violence and other serious discipline problems decreased. Referrals to the principal were reduced by 60 per cent. Generally, the most frequent conflicts were found to result from gossip/rumour, harassment, arguments, threats of physical violence, and negative behaviour in the classroom. Johnson et al. (1994) found that 92 first- to sixth-grade pupils, in four multi-age classes in an American suburban middle-class elementary school, were able to transfer the procedures and skills to their own peer conflicts, having participated in a peer mediation training programme. Prior to the training programme, which took place over six weeks for 30 minutes a day, frequent conflicts were reported involving academic work, physical aggression, playground activities, access to or possession of objects, turn-taking and put-downs and teasing. Careful observation of hallways, the dining room, the playground and the gymnasium revealed that four months after the training pupils seriously and carefully used their training to resolve highly emotional and prolonged conflicts with their peers. The frequency of student–student conflicts that teachers had to manage dropped by 80 per cent after the training, and the number of conflicts referred to the principal was reduced to zero.

In New Zealand, staff from 12 Auckland schools who set up peer mediation programmes describe the changes that they saw (Duncan, 1993):

> 'I don't have so many children rushing up to me on duty'; 'I often hear the children say "Let's find the mediators, they'll help"'; 'Incidents have lessened in the playground, children are much more responsible'; 'Mediators take their job seriously and excellent training has helped them to "solve" many types of problems. I am impressed with how they handle situations. I have not yet had to step in'.

One of the principals of the schools describes the concerns that led him to initiate a peer mediation programme:

> My concern was always that the children's problems were not being addressed at earlier stages, and occasionally incidents of "bullying" would emerge which could have been caught if the child concerned had someone to take that problem to other than a duty teacher. (p. 2)

After the peer mediation service was implemented, he notes a change:

> The difference as I see it is that children, particularly the younger ones, feel more secure in the playground. They now know where to take their problems and be heard. My deputy principal follows through the reports and discusses any patterns or concerns arising. These days the discussions are few and far between as the incidents are becoming minor. The older children have learned skills to empower them to deal with their peers. Therefore I have my schedule back! (p. 3)

Stacey and Robinson (1997) give a number of examples of teacher and pupil evaluations. The behaviour co-ordinator of a Birmingham primary school says:

> Mediation began as an aspect of school life, a taught element, and has become something which they use as part of their everyday lives, as useful as language and maths. Their skills at whatever level, have extended into their homes and lives outside school. (p. 157)

The headteacher of the school adds:

> We were looking for ways to further enhance our behaviour policy when we first became involved with mediation. . . . Our first mediators were brilliant. It was wonderful to watch them grow in confidence as the scheme got underway and was successful. Our third group of mediators has just started. The children never fail to amaze us. They get better every year. . . . The whole process of mediation has made a huge difference to our school. We find it almost impossible to say exactly why it has worked so well. It is a combination of many things. Perhaps the most important is that we did it as a whole school. I can't imagine our school without mediation. We feel really proud of what our children have achieved using the process of mediation. (p. 158)

The author's PhD research involved evaluating the effectiveness of a peer mediation programme in three primary schools in Birmingham. A quasi-experiment involving pupil questionnaires and teacher interviews was used to measure changes in levels of bullying, and levels of pupil self-esteem and locus of control, following peer mediation training of Year 5 (age 9 years) and the setting up of a peer mediation scheme. In School One the peer mediation programme coincided with the following changes:

- There was a reduction in the frequency of pupils reporting being a victim of bullying.
- There was a reduction in the frequency of pupils reporting bullying others.
- Types of bullying that appeared to reduce were physical bullying, teasing and psychological bullying.
- Pupil self-esteem improved after an initial dip, which suggests that pupils were undergoing some far-reaching reassessment of their self-concepts.
- Pupil feelings of empowerment improved.
- Pupils developed more negative attitudes towards bullying.
- After the peer mediation training programme, pupils had improved their ability to resolve conflicts, to give and receive positive comments, to co-operate, to communicate, and to listen to each other. By the time the peer mediation scheme had been running for two terms, they were beginning to transfer these skills to situations outside of the classroom, and many pupils had developed a high level of competency in these areas.

- Pupils with emotional and behavioural difficulties appeared to gain a great deal from this approach, with all pupils benefiting from a general reduction in disaffection and aggressive behaviour.

In School One, there was a whole-school approach with extensive staff training. The programme built on a negotiated, well-established code of conduct and reward system, and pupils were consulted about decisions that would affect their daily lives in many different ways. The headteacher and teachers appeared keen to hear about, and act on, instances of bullying, and modelled the mediation process themselves in their dealings with conflict in the classroom and playground. Pupils were able to practise personal, social and conflict resolution skills in real situations, and this led to a positive school culture. In particular, the headteacher had realistically assessed the starting-points and training needs of the pupils and staff.

In the other two schools, no peer mediation service was set up following the peer mediation training, and there were no apparent changes in pupil levels of bullying, self-esteem and locus of control. In these two schools, the programme was limited to Year 5 and the headteachers appeared to overestimate the skill level of their staff in solving conflicts without confrontation. It also appeared that pupils were sometimes discouraged from talking about bullying, with victims ignored or blamed by some teachers. Structured lessons, teacher control and playground supervision were used as anti-bullying strategies, and negative behaviour was at times excused on the grounds of supposed lack of parental skill and support. The code of 'conduct & reward' schemes was still being formulated in both schools.

Conclusion

Although more research into this area is needed, it does appear that peer mediation can have a positive effect on levels of bullying, self-esteem and locus of control amongst primary-age pupils. It also appears to have a beneficial effect on their personal, social and conflict-resolution skills. Caution does, however, need to be applied, as mediation is a sophisticated process with a rich social and psychological history. If misunderstood, or misapplied, its benefits may be lost, and, at worst, children may be set up for failure. In the author's experience children make wonderful mediators. It is invariably adults who need to review their attitudes towards conflict, power and control if peer mediation in a school setting is to thrive.

3

ELLIOTT DURHAM SCHOOL'S ANTI-BULLYING PEER SUPPORT SYSTEM: A CASE STUDY OF GOOD PRACTICE IN A SECONDARY SCHOOL

Paul Naylor

Elliott Durham is a mixed comprehensive school for some 460 11 to 16-year-old pupils taught by 30 teachers. It serves St Ann's, a disadvantaged inner-city ward in Nottingham (UK). Sixty-three per cent of the pupils are eligible for free school meals, 60 per cent are from single-parent families, 40 per cent are on the school's special educational needs register and over 80 per cent enter the school with reading ages below their chronological age (OFSTED, 1998). Furthermore, pupils' attainment is well below national average standards. In 1998, 10 per cent of the school's Year 11 (15 to 16-year-old) pupils gained five or more GCSE grades A* to C whilst the national average was 46.3 per cent (DfEE, 1999).

School ethos and role modelling by teachers

Despite the socially and economically disadvantaged backgrounds of many of its pupils, the school enjoys good relationships, as the OFSTED (1998, para. 49) report suggests:

> The school has been successful in establishing an ethos of mutual valuing and respect. . . . The respectful attitude and sensitive management [of pupils] by all staff sets an ethos in which pupils learn to value everyone's contribution. . . .

The adult interview respondents confirmed these views of relationships within the school. For example, Naomi Posner, head of modern languages, said:

... the teachers are excellent models. Senior management makes it quite clear that all handling of pupils should be done in a calm manner, and shouting is out in this school. Pupils are treated with the utmost respect. . . .

Adrian Dyer, classroom assistant, endorses this view:

We've got a very understanding staff. I've never seen teachers bullying pupils, and I've been in virtually every classroom.

The interviewed peer supporters also confirmed that there are no teachers in the school who bully pupils.

Terry Whysall, deputy headteacher, suggests that the adults in the school need to be seen by the pupils to present the models of pro-social behaviour which they expect the peer support system to promote. She also expresses the view that it is difficult to envisage that a peer support system would be successful in a school environment in which relationships were typified by autocracy.

If you're trying to put a scheme like this into a hierarchical school system, I think you'd work yourself into the ground.

Carrying out a needs analysis

Although the school has well-articulated code of conduct and an equal opportunities policy, of which all of the Year 7 and 9 (ages 11–12 years and 13–14 years) interview respondents showed a sound knowledge and understanding, an important reason for setting up the system is explained by Robin Tinker, teacher in charge of the peer support system:

In the bullying lessons I was doing with Year 7 pupils, the message we were preaching was, 'If you have any hassle, you must tell someone', and we didn't think that was happening.

A Year 7 interviewee explains why some pupils are reluctant to tell teachers about their peer relationship problems:

Teachers tell other teachers and they might make it worse by shouting at them [the bullies] and then they might do it more.

And these Year 9 pupils suggest some other reasons:

Bullied pupils might not think a teacher will understand properly and they'd rather speak to someone of their own age . . . [but] . . . not a friend who they might fall out with [and who] might go round telling everyone.

Parents take it in to their own hands and start blabbing about it. They will be overprotective and might not understand that you don't want them to do that . . . so they might actually make things worse.

However, Robin was aware that the idea would need support from the school community as a whole:

You've got to have support of your governors, . . . your senior management team, . . . staff, children and . . . parents.

Consequently, meetings about the possibility of Elliott Durham having a support system were held with the school's senior managers, some of the teachers and ancillary staff and some of the pupils. The pupils were consulted in a number of meetings, including those with:

- a democratically elected sample of the pupils from across the school's age range;
- the members of the school council;
- the pupil representatives on the school's governing body.

The school's senior managers also agreed with Robin's suggestion that the idea for a peer support system in Elliott Durham should be debated by the staff during part of an INSET (IN-Service Education and Training) day. In the course of this day, Robin and the school counsellor, Meryl Salt, were very open:

We can't do it unless you're willing to support us, and you're willing to pilot it for a couple of terms.

The outcome of the meetings and the INSET session was that the school agreed to pilot a peer support system, although there were some anxieties about the risks that they were taking on. Meryl summarized these fears as follows:

There . . . can be difficulties about . . . teachers worrying about what's going to happen: 'Is there going to be a big risk?' I think all of us were very aware of the risks involved and we were all scared when we took it on board: 'Is it going to be positive?' 'Is something going to go wrong?'

The school's experience suggests that the successful implementation of a peer support system depends on careful planning and research, debate between governors, teachers, parents and pupils, and the careful selection and training of the peer supporters. It is also clear that these processes can take many months.

Management of the system

Derek Wilson, the school's educational psychologist, Meryl, Robin and Terry are the four adults who are directly involved in managing the system with the active support of the overwhelming majority of the school's staff. Derek and Meryl, as the professional counsellors, are responsible for selecting, training and supervising the peer supporters, whilst Robin has the day-to-day responsibility for managing, administering and monitoring the system under the oversight of Terry. Each of these people therefore has a clearly defined role in the system and acts together co-operatively with the others. Derek describes the model of peer support used in the anti-bullying campaign (ABC) system as: 'Client-led, non-directive'.

Selection, training, appointment and supervision of the peer supporters

Selection

Meryl and Derek, and the peer supporters, have a carefully thought-out set of criteria for selecting pupils to become trainee peer supporters. The selection process is rigorous. Prospective peer supporters from Year 8 and above are invited to complete an application form (Box 3.1).

The completed candidates' forms are short-listed by Derek and Meryl and the existing peer supporters on 'the basis of how convincingly they've completed' them (Derek). In some schools, there is a reluctance to give the peer-supporting task to anybody younger than a sixth former (Year 12 or 13, 16–19 years old) because they are not considered 'mature enough'. But Meryl questions the basis of using this criterion on the grounds that to a Year 7 pupil, a sixth former, for example, may be just as forbidding as an adult.

> The youngest peer supporter that we have [had] was Year 8 when we took her on [and she] dealt with the majority of Year 7s. They found it easier to relate to someone of their age. . . . I think the age gap from Year 7 to 11 would have been too much for some pupils. . . .

Short-listed candidates are interviewed. The interviewing panel, consisting of Derek, the peer supporters and sometimes Meryl, seeks responses to open-ended questions such as the following:

- Think of a time when you turned to someone for help or support. Describe how it felt to approach that person.
- If you are appointed, you will be working as a member of a peer support group. What do you think it takes to be an effective group member?
- Is there anything you'd like to add or ask us?

Derek outlines the criteria which are used in selecting interviewees for training:

Box 3.1 *The ABC application form*

Elliott Durham School
ABC **Application Form**

Name: _____   Tutor Set: _____

Year: _____   Sex(Male/female): _____

Why do you want to become a peer supporter?

_____

_____

Would you say that your friends think that you are a good peer supporter?

_____

_____

Have you ever been bullied or been a bully? (Please give details)

_____

_____

As a peer supporter, what do you think you would be good at?

_____

_____

Can you think of anything that's hard about peer supporting?

_____

_____

Who do you think the scheme is for?

_____

_____

Are you good at taking responsibility? (Give an example.)

_____

_____

Would you say you could keep confidentiality?

_____

_____

Signature _____   Date _____

Please return to the school office in the envelope provided.

... we're looking for ... pupils who can say something reasonably coherent in the interview setting ... [which] is hard for them to do. ... Anybody who manages to get any sort of narrative together [around the interview questions] ... has got a good chance of being chosen.

And Meryl adds:

We haven't chosen the ones who are totally [concerned with] advice-giving [even though they] really care.

None of the school's teachers is involved in the selection process of the peer supporters. Only the adult 'outsiders', Meryl and Derek, engage in this process. Meryl spells out the reason for this practice:

... if the peer supporters were dealing with difficult issues that they would find it difficult to relate to teachers, it would be easier telling someone from outside the school even though we are bound by the same rules on confidentiality. ...

However, the empowerment of the peer supporters by involving them in selecting the trainee peer supporters has not been without its problems. Robin, from his perspective as a teacher in the school, agrees:

We've got preconceived ideas and when a couple of names first appeared, I had doubts. But that's me in my other role. I have to step out of it a little and trust their judgement.

Derek explores the issue of bias raised in some of the interviews:

Where there have been tensions is where people have applied who have an existing bad relationship with one of the peer supporters: 'I'm not in it, if he's going to be in it', sort of feeling. We've had to spend time helping them draw the boundary between being somebody's friend and liking them and being a colleague in a team and trying to make it clear that you don't have to like somebody to work well together. It's almost part of the training ... sort of culturing into being a bit professional.

So Derek argues that problems arising from poor relationships between peer supporters can be turned into opportunities for their personal and social development.

A history of bad behaviour is not in itself a reason for excluding a pupil from consideration to become a trainee peer supporter.

I would be ... more interested in somebody who looked like they might have a bit of a reputation. ... But if it was somebody who was very inadequate, ... in trouble for non-attending and not for causing trouble or being mouthy ... and with very little evident personality, I don't think they'd be the right choice. It isn't a scheme for rehabilitating inadequate kids. It sounds anti-egalitarian ... but I'm very clear in my own mind that you're aiming to recruit the kids

... who've got big 'cred', are shiny, attractive and who people will think that if they're doing it then it must be a good thing. . . . Often they'll be a bit naughty but you need the 'cred' that they bring with them. You can't always get them to apply, but when you can, I very much want to get them on to training and see what we can do. (Derek)

Unusually, for many mixed-sex schools which have a peer support system (Naylor and Cowie, 1999), Elliott Durham has succeeded in achieving a gender balance amongst the peer supporters:

We've always had enough boys to make it reasonable. I wasn't aware until quite recently that . . . this tends to be a feminine activity. Maybe it was down to the first year when we did have enough boys and it's always been part of the mindset in the school that this is something that boys do. . . . It's . . . part of the culture of the school. (Derek)

A possible reason for the gender balance in the peer supporters is the 'ethos of care' permeating the school, which has been discussed earlier. Another possibility is that the gender balance amongst the system's management team – two women and two men – has influenced the pupils and teachers in the school into believing that peer support is not an activity which is exclusively associated with one or the other gender. Again, this may be another example of the way in which pupils in the school are influenced by the behaviour which they see significant adults modelling for them.

Training and appointment

The training of the peer supporters is also carefully thought out and thorough. Successful interviewees are invited to attend training sessions run by Meryl and Derek. Only on the successful completion of this training are these interviewees appointed as peer supporters. In Meryl's terms, the aims of the initial training are:

Basically listening skills . . . and we are very clear, . . . pupils are only dealing with bullying issues.

In this statement, Meryl highlights another positive feature of the system, which is that it has a clearly defined focus, namely bullying, which is made clear to the peer supporters and the users of the system.

Meryl also has clear objectives about what the training should enable the pupils to do:

. . . not to overtrain. We were very aware . . . that if we took the pupils too far into counselling skills they may try to handle more than we might want them to. . . . We felt that all we needed is practice, practice and practice after we've given these basics. . . .

Derek added that the key processes by which this 'limited objective' training is achieved are through 'joint-action' and role-playing:

> We do it jointly. I guess we try to model something by doing it jointly . . . peer support isn't something you do by yourself in this context. . . . We're always encouraging work in pairs with pupils. . . . We also coach role-plays.

In terms of time, as Derek explains, the training is extensive:

> We do . . . a full afternoon of school time and then four one-hour twilight sessions. We're aiming to build in the basics. Over the last couple of years I've used a large wall graphic that's . . . a huge sheet of paper and . . . by the end of the fourth twilight session it's got everything we have talked about and all of their comments.

When asked about the advice that the peer supporters are given about how to tackle problems that are brought to them, Meryl said:

> . . . go no further than listening, reflecting and seeing if pupils will actually come to myself, or a teacher, if there's something more needed. . . .

The following comment by a peer supporter clearly demonstrates that he has internalized the 'client-led, non-directive' model of peer support described by Derek and Meryl:

> You don't actually solve their problem. You try and get them to think of ways they can sort . . . it out. . . . We help them solve it.

And the following conversation between the interviewer and a peer supporter also shows that he knows that he should be non-judgemental:

> I: Do you ever think to yourself: 'I'm listening to what this person is telling me and . . . I really don't think this is bullying'?
> PS: Everyone has their own different ways of classing things as bullying and not bullying.

Regarding 'rules' of confidentiality, Meryl had this to say about the peer supporters:

> . . . they are taught that anything they can't handle must come to myself or Derek and if it's child abuse it will go to someone straight away.

The thoroughness of the peer supporters' training was tested when a girl came to one peer supporter with a difficult issue to disclose. It was immediately passed on to an adult. Meryl reflects on this case in this way:

> . . . the team acknowledged that it was a real positive, even though it was a difficult situation, because it demonstrated that what we had taught the children had gone through.

The peer supporters are trained to make it clear to users that they must pass on to an adult in the school all serious non-bullying matters. The professionalism of the peer supporters regarding the issue of confidentiality was confirmed by the fact that users unanimously stated that they had never had a confidence betrayed by a peer supporter.

Supervision

Another strength of the *ABC* system concerns the regular supervision of the peer supporters. Group supervision meetings lasting for 30 minutes are held every week during a lunchtime and facilitated by Robin or Terry and either Meryl or Derek. Unnamed individual cases are discussed during which supporters occasionally seek advice and disseminate ideas on, for example, appropriate or successful approaches. These meetings are also used for the dissemination and discussion of *ABC* administrative business such as that about forthcoming 'in-service' training events and the selection of the next cohort of supporters.

How pupils access the system

One of the peer supporters explained how pupils access the system:

> There's a box near reception and . . . a pupil . . . puts a note in it to say who they want to see. The peer supporters empty the box, and if it's got a slip in it for them, they put an appointment slip in that pupil's register. Then the *ABC* peer support room is booked and you bring them into the room and help them get through it.

Robin explained why an appointment system as opposed to a 'drop-in' service was chosen:

> The first group of peer supporters . . . said it's got to be confidential. They won't want to be seen coming to peer supporters.

However, Robin went on to elaborate that the appointments system is but one of the ways in which pupils now access the system:

> . . . we're finding more children are approaching peer supporters personally. That's how we're getting about 45 per cent referrals. Another 45 per cent are through the appointment system. . . . The other 10 per cent are from teachers referring. Now that skews the confidentiality issue. We've talked about it and said we would accept referrals like that. . . .

Terry also comments on the way in which some teachers refer pupils to the *ABC* system:

Teachers are saying: 'It would be a good idea if you did make an appointment.' The two systems of adult support and peer support are getting enmeshed. I don't think we've got a predetermined idea of how it will grow. . . . It's more this is how it's developing for us and the needs of our children.

Thus, the system is sensitive to the perceived changes in the needs of the schools' teachers and pupils.

How pupils access the peer support room without being noticed by other pupils, and even teachers, is a problem which confronts most schools. At Elliott Durham, this problem has been carefully thought through in the ways spelled out in the following interview conversation with the peer supporters:

I: Let's suppose that you've arranged to meet somebody in the peer support room. Whilst you're walking up the stairs and along the corridor there might be lots of other pupils who've seen you with this person and they might say, 'Oh, that person has got a problem.'

PS: That's why we send them up first while we get the key. And we hide the key. . . .

I: But if they see someone walk through that door isn't it obvious that they're going to see a peer supporter?

PS: Well, this room is used for many other things. It's used for teachers' meetings, open days, a tea room for parents' evenings and the inspectors [OFSTED] used it, . . . and when pupils have a problem.

This simple idea of using the room for a variety of purposes significantly reduces the chances (by comparison with a dedicated peer support room) that users of the system will be readily identifiable.

Number of peer supporters

A problem perceived by supporters and teachers who run systems in many schools is that the service is underused (Naylor and Cowie, 1999). Typically, the supporters and teachers who run systems report that there are not enough users to maintain the supporters' interest and enthusiasm. With this observation in mind, the optimum number of supporters was discussed with Robin:

I: You currently have 10 peer supporters and you're saying that by the summer it could be down to five. I have been in a school where they've got 40 peer supporters. Is there something that I don't know here?

R: When we started, we had 16 . . . and there just wasn't enough for them to do. They were really enthusiastic and they did a load of publicity . . . but they weren't getting the cases. . . . By May, the eight Year 11 [15 to 16-year-olds] ones had gone, we were left with eight Year 10 [14 to 15-year-olds] and we found that much easier to work with so we said: 'Right, we don't need those big numbers.'

Robin raises an important issue in this comment. Through careful monitoring of the use of the service (see below), the managers and peer supporters have taken the pragmatic decision to reduce the number of peer supporters through 'natural wastage' and thereby create a better balance between 'need' and 'provision'. Such 'needs analysis' is based on the outcomes of the regular supervision that the peer supporters receive, which has been discussed earlier, and from the records of the use of the system that Robin keeps.

As Robin points out, however, it is always possible to make good use of 'non-peer support' help from some pupils in running a peer support system:

> One lad was an absolute whiz on the computer. We . . . trained him as a peer supporter but he didn't make it. So we said: 'Can we attach you to *ABC* and give you stuff to type up and make a poster out of it?' But he wasn't a peer supporter, . . . a secretary if you like.

Monitoring and evaluating the system

One of Robin's key tasks in the management of the system is that of monitoring and evaluating its effectiveness. He does this through maintaining a list of unnamed users of the service, which, he acknowledges, is probably incomplete because of the confidential nature of the service. However, at the end of the 1997 autumn term, in a written report to the school staff, he was able to say:

> This term, *ABC* has handled 18 cases involving 20 pupil victims, the greatest number we have had. . . . All were Year 7 and 8 pupils. This makes a total of 47 cases and 62 pupils since the service began. . . .

He went on to interpret this use of the system in the following terms:

> It seems that pupils are much more ready to 'tell' about bullying, and this may be due to the 'culture' of *ABC*. . . . Its main clients are younger pupils, Years 7 and 8, roughly a 50:50 male/female split. . . . There are peaks and troughs within the year. . . . This time of year is very flat, just before Easter. Just before Christmas the peer supporters were rushed off their feet. . . . A lot of Year 7 go to peer supporters in their second half term here. . . . This is because we do a lesson with them about *ABC* in Personal, Social and Health Education (PSHE) at the end of September.

Robin also conducts an annual questionnaire survey of all of the pupils and teachers in the school. The pupil questionnaires ask for responses to a number of questions which test pupils' knowledge of the system and their attitudes towards it. Responses reveal that pupils have a very good knowledge of the school's system. These pupils said that they had learned about the school's *ABC* system in PSE lessons, in assemblies, from posters around the school and from letters to their parents. Confirmation that Year 7 and 9 pupils are generally well informed about the *ABC* system comes from the research questionnaire and interview responses on which this case study is based.

Promoting the system outside of the school

The *ABC* system has been promoted beyond the school in a number of ways. All of the peer supporters speak to parents and children from the school's feeder primary schools (for 5 to 11-year-olds) at 'open evenings'. Some of the peer supporters also visit the feeder primary schools with Terry, where they speak to pupils about the school's *ABC* scheme. Three of the peer supporters helped to facilitate an INSET event in July 1997 for teachers and other Nottinghamshire local education authority professionals.

Robin and the peer supporters have also recently had published an article on the school's system (Tinker, 1998).

Summary

The Elliott Durham School *ABC* system represents good practice for the following reasons:

- It has the strong support of the school's governors and senior managers, the majority of the teachers, parents and pupils who are well informed about the system.
- The system was established only after careful planning and consultation with all of the interested groups of people.
- It is well managed by a co-operative team of adults each of whom has a clearly defined and understood role in the running of the system.
- The school has been imaginative in electing to use much of its educational psychologist's time in developing the system for the benefit of the whole school community rather than on individual pupil casework. It has also chosen to use some of the part-time counsellor's time in this way. In these respects, the school has chosen to shift the focus from 'cure' to 'prevention'.
- The selection, training and supervision of the peer supporters are carefully thought out, thorough and meet standards of good professional counselling practice.
- The system has a clearly defined and limited function which is understood by all, particularly by the supporters and users of the system.
- It is positively promoted both within and outside the school and its successes are justifiably celebrated.

- The views and ideas about and attitudes towards the system of the peer supporters, teachers and potential and actual users are regularly sought and acted on so that the system is sensitive to changes which are perceived to be necessary.
- All aspects of the confidentiality issue have been carefully considered so that 'mistakes' are unlikely to happen.

Acknowledgements

Thanks are due to the questionnaire and interview respondents for their time. This research was funded by the Prince's Trust.

PART II

DEVELOPING A PEER SUPPORT SERVICE

4

PLANNING A PEER SUPPORT SERVICE

In writing this section, which we think of as the 'how to' section of the book, it seems important first to explain the background to our approach. We have a wide range of experience of setting up, managing and monitoring peer support services in schools and in the community, in Britain and abroad. Based on this experience, we have now run several trainings – for teachers, youth workers, social workers and other people concerned with the welfare of children and young people – on setting up peer support services. In the process of running these trainings, we have learned from the knowledge and experience of our students, many of whom now manage peer support services themselves. We have also had the advantage of input from other trainers in this area, notably Trevor Cole from Canada, who kindly offered us the use of the peer support training exercises in his book *Kids Helping Kids* (1987), and Fiona Macbeth, who trained us both in the LEAP model of conflict resolution. In addition, we are informed by our years of experience as counsellors, lecturers and trainers. In this context it is worth mentioning that some of the training exercises we will suggest in later chapters come from the wider counselling training field. Some we have known of for so long that we cannot remember where they first came from; many others we have simply created ourselves as the need arose.

The practical sections of this book offer ideas that have been tried (with varying degrees of success!) in the real world. There is no 'right' or infallible way to go about planning a peer support service. However, in these next few chapters, our intention is to offer some ideas and practical advice that we believe will increase your chances of ending up with a successful, sustainable peer support service.

Where do I start?

Peer support starts with an awareness of need and the desire to find a way of meeting that need. The usual reason that people want to learn about peer support is that they have a true concern about the needs of children and young people. Most often they are working in a capacity that allows them access to the feelings, needs or experiences with which young people struggle. They then often look for solutions within the professional system and find that the service they need is not available, the resources are not available to 'purchase' the service, or perhaps, having accessed a professional, they discover that a 'professional' was not the solution after all.

From awareness of need to planning an intervention

Having become aware of a need/problem, at first sight it seems sensible to move towards looking for a solution or intervention that may help the young people involved. However, in our experience, one of the reasons peer support services struggle or fail is because someone, with all the best intentions, has moved too quickly to an apparent solution without first clearly assessing the situation. Our response to this situation is the use of a needs analysis.

What is a needs analysis?

Quite simply, a needs analysis is a structured and reasonably objective approach to identifying the needs of a particular group, assessing the resources available to meet those needs and planning an appropriate intervention.

Why a needs analysis?

There are three different but equally important reasons for doing a needs analysis. The first and most obvious is to discover the scope of the needs/ problems in order to plan the most suitable intervention to address these needs/problems. An intervention that works is most likely to be based on a full understanding of the problem, of the resources available to address the problem, and of the possible difficulties in so doing. A needs analysis provides a structured way of finding out this information and then of making decisions and plans based upon it.

The second purpose is to begin early on the process of involving other relevant people (staff, young people, parents) in planning, developing and participating in the peer support service. 'Ownership' of the service by all relevant parties is absolutely essential if lack of support for or even sabotage of the peer support service is to be avoided.

And, third, it is important to emphasize here our commitment to modelling the practice we intend to encourage in others. Thus we feel that if we aim to encourage young people to work co-operatively to achieve an environment that works better for everyone, then we too should be committed to and demonstrate co-operative working. The needs analysis provides the first opportunity to demonstrate co-operative working, with all its strengths and weaknesses.

Are there any disadvantages to the process of needs analysis?

Despite its many advantages, there are always difficulties to planning a service co-operatively. However, it is as well to get used to them early in the process as you will surely encounter them from time to time throughout the development and management of the service!

One common problem is the difficulty getting people, or some groups of people, to respond to your requests for involvement. Whilst many people may express an interest in your ideas, many fewer of those same people will attend a meeting to give their views or fill in a questionnaire. In the multicultural context of most schools and youth projects today, it is worth giving some thought as to whether and why some groups of people are excluded or exclude themselves from giving their views and finding ways to access that information. It is quite likely that these are the individuals or groups most in need of involvement in the peer support service.

Even if a wide range of participants take part, it is likely that you will receive conflicting information. For example, in some schools, a large number of students may tell you of the prevalence of bullying whilst the teaching staff or board of governors may deny its existence. Whilst awareness of these conflicting views may make it difficult to take the next step of planning an intervention, it is still better to know about the range of perspectives than to develop a service on the incorrect assumption that everyone is in agreement. Given that information, it may be possible, for example, to plan a 'compromise' intervention which is effective and upon which all parties can agree. It may be necessary to work to influence the views of one or more of the parties before introducing any intervention. Either way, it is best to know the position you are starting from before you begin.

Perhaps the most difficult situation for someone committed to developing a service to improve the school or community environment is when the findings of the needs analysis contradict his or her own beliefs/views. It can be an unpleasant surprise to realize that others do not share your often strongly held views on what the problems are or what is to be done about them. We have known people to choose different solutions in this situation, as described in Examples 4.1 and 4.2.

Example 4.1

One school counsellor decided, based upon discussions with some of the older students, that a peer support service would be a good idea in the school in which she worked. She had an idea that groups of younger students led by two or three older students would be a good forum for discussing any problems the younger students were having. However, when she asked the students and teachers using questionnaires, the response was that the younger students would be more likely to talk to someone they know on a one-to-one basis. Nevertheless, after some consideration, the counsellor decided that as a counsellor she 'knew better' than the students and teachers how to handle difficult emotional issues, and she continued with her original plans despite the findings of her 'needs analysis'. Unsurprisingly, she had difficulty gaining co-operation at the implementation stage of her service. Older students did not feel confident to lead the groups of younger students; younger students felt too exposed, and, instead of raising problems in the group, came to see the peer supporters later; and teachers did not have confidence in the groups and so did not prioritize their students' attendance. In the end this peer support service failed.

Example 4.2

A teacher who was doing a counselling course in her spare time decided that something needed to be done about the levels of bullying in the school. Her first thought was that a listening service, based on a counselling model, would be helpful. However, when she asked the young people about this, they said that a formal service would be too intimidating to younger students and they would prefer something more informal. The teacher then planned, with the students, a befriending service where each new student was paired with an older student and the young people decided between them where and when they would meet. This teacher recognized that she had wanted a counselling-based service more because of her own interests than because it was necessarily the best service for the school. This service became a fixture within the school.

There is no point in doing a needs analysis if you do not intend to use the findings to guide the planning and development of your service. As one of the peer support attitudes we will be helping young people to develop is the ability to respect or at least tolerate difference, it is essential that we do our best to 'hear' and to accommodate views and ideas which differ from our own. Even at this stage in the process, we can model working co-operatively with colleagues and students. It is important to remember that your attitude and behaviour in this early stage will influence how people understand the entire process of peer support and how they respond to your interventions.

In the next section, we describe a nine-step format for structuring a needs analysis.

Structuring a needs analysis

Step 1: The setting

Organizational 'culture' is probably the most influential aspect of the setting in terms of setting up a peer support service, and there are two issues that arise quite often. One is the issue of hierarchy versus democracy. Essentially, if the peer support 'culture' of empowerment of young people to help themselves runs counter to the prevailing 'culture' of decision-making and control from the top, then this will need to be taken into account when deciding whether or not a peer support service can work in that setting.

The other is the issue of force versus co-operation. If the, often unspoken, organizational culture is one of bullying (whether physical or verbal) staff and/or young people into compliance, then it is unlikely to be receptive to the 'counter-culture' of peer support which speaks out against bullying and in favour of co-operation and tolerance. It may be that those of you who are working with young people will not be surprised when I suggest that in some schools and organizations a bullying culture comes from the top downwards, as shown in Example 4.3.

Example 4.3

We were asked to train a group of peer supporters in a secondary school with a high level of violence and bullying. On the first morning of the three-day training, we worked with the young people on developing an ethos of dealing with conflict non-aggressively and finding 'win–win' solutions. On coming out of the hall for our lunch break, we encountered a scene that illuminated one of the reasons for this school's problems. In the corridor, observed by many students, was a senior member of the teaching staff shouting abuse and pinning a student to the wall by his throat! Whilst few organizations in these litigation-conscious times will demonstrate the roots of their problems so graphically, it is worth bearing in mind that similar attitudes can lie hidden just under the surface and still powerfully influence the organizational culture.

The existence of conflicting 'cultures' does not mean a peer support service cannot work. In fact, as the illustration above shows, it may be one of the reasons it is needed. In my experience, there are two possible ways forward. One is to address the culture conflict head-on but as diplomatically as you can manage (and begin practising your conflict-resolution skills from the start!) The other is to develop strategies to circumvent the issue. For example, developing a peer support service based on befriending would be less likely to provoke difficulties than developing a conflict-resolution service which directly confronts the organization's own issues. It is important not to get caught up in the belief that addressing the conflict directly is the only true solution. As you will discover in later sections on training peer supporters, a solution that people have the skills and willingness to use is probably the best solution for them in that situation.

Step 2: The people

It is important to know something about your colleagues, the young people and possibly their parents before you develop a peer support service, as they will constitute your best resource, the users of your service and your main source of resistance. Whether you have a very mixed demographic situation or a fairly homogeneous group, perhaps the most important question to ask yourself is: 'How do I best access the resources of this/these group(s)?' It is essential to look first at positive attributes. Many of the people with whom and for whom you will be developing this peer support service are used to being seen as having little to offer. For this reason, you need to believe in them yourself and signal early on that you and peer support have a different approach.

You do, of course, need to consider whether there are any particular problems existing within (for example, poor literacy) or between (for example, racism) these groups. With a little creative thinking, some problems are fairly easily dealt with, as Example 4.4 demonstrates.

Example 4.4

One peer support programme was developed on a housing estate known for high levels of crime and poverty. Knowing that many young people on the estate had problems with literacy, this service trained its peer supporters to do face-to-face interviews in which young people's views could be obtained verbally and the peer supporter could write them down. This was a creative approach in that it was a needs analysis which did not require literacy and in that it provided an opportunity for peer supporters to introduce themselves to the young people who might use their service.

A final word about demographics: if you or the peer supporters come from a different cultural background (culture is used in the wide sense here to include race, religion, gender, sexuality, class, and so on) than the young people you hope to work with, there is likely to be some difficulty with the credibility of the service. Ideally a peer support service will have supporters from the same range of cultural backgrounds as the people using the service. However, this does not necessarily mean that people using the service should be paired with a supporter from their cultural group. The issue is choice. It should be possible to choose to speak to someone who is familiar with one's own culture, but it should never be assumed that this is the best alternative. Example 4.5 illustrates how not consulting potential service-users on this matter can result in the failure of the service.

Example 4.5

A health and support service was set up for young people with HIV/AIDS from a particular ethnic background. These young people were often ill, isolated and depressed. Many of them were refugees, sometimes without any family in the UK. In an attempt to reduce their social isolation, the team providing the professional services decided to develop a peer support service in which other young people from that ethnic background would be recruited to 'buddy' them. A great deal of effort was put into finding suitable 'buddies', not easy at a time when HIV/AIDS held terrible stigma within that community. However, when the first meeting of the buddies and their partners was arranged, none of the young people with HIV/AIDS came. When the reasons for this were explored, the young people said that they did not want to have buddies from the same ethnic group in case information about their illness got back to people in their own countries. They were concerned that this would negatively affect the work and marriage prospects of their family members. However, when young British peer supporters were recruited, the service was very well used.

In conclusion, if the service is to succeed, it is very important that it address and be seen to address the needs of all communities.

Step 3: The issues

Before developing a service, you will need to find out about the problems faced by the young people with whom you plan to work. To investigate these problems, some consultation is necessary. The difficulty lies in deciding whom to ask and how and what to ask them. The obvious people to ask are the young people themselves. In addition, it is informative and tactful to ask staff in the organization where you expect to run the peer support service. Some schools, particularly primary schools, also choose to ask parents' views. You are likely to find that ideas differ amongst the three groups as to what the most significant problems are, and you will need to address these differences when you prioritize which problems your peer support service will work on.

Initial consultation is often carried out through use of questionnaires and group discussion or focus groups brainstorming the problem. Questionnaires need to be designed with the language and literacy levels of the proposed respondents in mind. They have the advantage of being anonymous and therefore more likely to produce honest and revealing responses. You can ensure a good return rate if time is given in class or at some other event and they are collected before people leave. A questionnaire 'taken home to complete' is less likely to be returned! Box 4.1 is a sample questionnaire which was used to consult teaching staff at a school. With a few adjustments, the same form can be used to consult parents and young people.

Group discussions, if well facilitated, can produce interesting and creative solutions. However, they often do not tap the experiences and ideas of the minority as it can be too exposing for most young people to express different or dissenting views in a forum of their peers.

The questions you ask depend on the amount of detailed information you want and you think you can get. In general, keeping a questionnaire brief and simple to complete is likely to increase your rate of return. We favour a two-tiered model of consultation. The first tier involves finding out which problems the young people are experiencing, and could also include asking how they would feel about using a peer-led service if it existed. You might also want to ask if the young people or the staff (or parents if you decide to include them) would have any particular concerns about using a peer support service, so that these concerns can be addressed in how the service is set up and marketed. The second tier of the consultation could be used to develop 'ownership' of the service, either by collating the findings and taking them back to public meetings where some ideas for a possible peer support service can be developed by the group, or by producing some ideas for a possible service based upon the information you received and then putting these out to consultation. On the whole, we have found people prefer action to consultation, so a little consultation can go a long way. On the other hand, a lack of consultation will almost certainly result in resistance. It is important that you find a balance between consultation and action which suits you and your setting.

Box 4.1   *Peer support: staff questionnaire*

1. Looking at the issues listed below, tick the ones that you think are of greatest concern to young people in your school.
   ☐ Achieving high grades
   ☐ Feelings of loneliness and exclusion
   ☐ Friendships
   ☐ Making career choices
   ☐ Bullying
   ☐ Family problems
   ☐ Drug or alcohol use
   ☐ Boyfriend/girlfriend relationships
   ☐ Relationships with teachers

2. Please add here any issues which were not on the list above, but which you consider to be important.

3. Of all the issues above, which three would you say need to be addressed most urgently.

   1.   2.   3.

4. To whom do you think young people talk most often about their personal concerns?
   ☐ Parents
   ☐ Teachers
   ☐ Friends
   ☐ School counsellor

5. Do you think peers are effective in helping each other deal with personal concerns? Why or why not?

6. Do you think young people could be trained to be more effective in helping other young people?

7. Do you think young people should have more involvement in creating a good environment in the school?

8. With which of the concerns listed above do you think trained young people could help other young people in the school?

Prioritizing is absolutely essential. A peer support service cannot be the solution to all problems. The danger of not prioritizing is that you try to develop a service to meet all needs and end up meeting none. In addition, you end up with a disillusioned group of peer supporters and possibly a number of colleagues saying 'I told you so.' Therefore, it is necessary to select from the many issues and problems that will be identified a small number or even just one which your peer support service will be designed to address. People tend to prioritize either according to urgency – that is, bullying is such a severe problem at our school that we must deal with that – or according to what is most likely to succeed – for example, a fairly straightforward buddying service for new pupils in a class. As you have asked a whole range of people which problems they think need addressing, you can expect them to want an explanation if you do not choose to address the problem they think is most significant. So be prepared! There is no right or wrong decision. Simply ensure that you know why you have made your decision and be willing to explain your process and reasoning if asked.

Step 4: Resources

It is quite usual for schools and other organizations to support the idea of a peer-led intervention as it is seen as a low- or, even, no-cost answer to quite significant problems. Our experience is that a well-run peer support programme is not without cost. At the very least, it costs the time and energy of the staff members who develop and manage it. They often do this in addition to their regular duties and without financial compensation. For the more complex, counselling-based services, there may be the need to 'buy-in' training and supervision. A room with privacy and a place to store records will also be needed. In gaining the support of the budget-holders for your project, it is important to be clear about the resources you will need to run the project effectively. If these are not forthcoming, then you will need to decide whether or not it is worth going ahead or whether you need to alter the type of peer support service you want to offer. Our observation is that the resource arena is one in which many an unspoken resistance is acted out. Example 4.6 describes one such situation.

Example 4.6

In the context of acting out resistance in the resource arena, a clear example is the headmaster who expressed his ambivalence about a new peer support service through his allocation of rooms. At first the peer support service was offered as their 'private' room, a room in which teachers kept their belongings and which as a result they were constantly entering during peer support sessions. When the teacher responsible for the peer support service complained about this lack of confidentiality, she was offered a room which happened to share a wall, in fact, a completely transparent *glass* wall, with the headmaster's office. It did not take tremendous interpretative ability to ascertain that the headmaster felt some need to 'keep his eye' on the peer support service! The result, of course, was that no one used the peer support service formally, but contacts were made in the corridors and the school grounds.

Step 5: Goals

At this point the major players in this venture need to have a shared set of goals. Ideally, the goals which you are trying to achieve will be agreed by the young people, the staff, the parents and any other funding or controlling bodies (for example, board of governors).

The idea of **SMART** goals comes from the Open University's Accounting for Managers programme (Parkinson 1999), but it applies equally well to goals set for other purposes.

Your goals need to be:
S – specific
M – measurable
A – achievable
R – realistic
T – to a time scale (adapted from Parkinson, 1999, p. 15)

SMART goals may be input- or outcome-focused. An example of a SMART input-focused goal would be: at least 12 students will meet with a peer supporter in the first 6 months the service is running. An example of an outcome-focused goal would be: students will report fewer incidents of lunch money being stolen by the end of the first year of the peer support service. (Clearly this desired outcome would require some measure of reported incidents of lunch money being stolen before the commencement of the peer support service and then again after one year.)

As indicated above, the point of clearly defining specific goals before you begin is so that you have a baseline against which to measure your progress. This will help in the monitoring and evaluation of your project.

Step 6: Potential roadblocks

The purpose of identifying potential roadblocks early on is either so that you can think of ways to circumvent them or, even better, so that you can find a way of getting them to work in your favour. Once you are able to identify a roadblock, it loses some of its power and you can begin to think of ways around it. When facing a human 'roadblock', it is worth remembering that within the person who combats you most actively lies the potential to be your most zealous supporter. Usually people block the progress of what is in many ways quite an innocuous intervention because it threatens them in some way. Help them feel less threatened and they will be on your side. The teacher in Example 4.7 was one such enemy-turned-supporter.

Example 4.7

Mr H. was well known as a rigid but well-meaning teacher. When the headteacher supported the idea of peer education on sexual health issues under the guidance of the school nurse, Mr H. expressed his reservations vociferously. The school nurse listened attentively to Mr H.'s concerns and addressed some of them in how she developed the peer support programme. Still Mr H. did all he could to sabotage the service. Finally when it came time to pilot the service, the school nurse decided to confront the problem directly and asked Mr H. if she could pilot it with his class. She said it would be very helpful if he could be present for the sessions with her so that he could help her in planning any necessary alterations. Mr H. agreed, apparently under duress from the headteacher. However, as he attended sessions and became involved in their development, Mr H. began to be 'converted' to the idea. By the end of the term, Mr H. was speaking just as loudly in favour of the peer education service as he had previously against it!

Remember too that the process of facing problems and finding solutions together is all 'grist for the mill' in a peer support service. Make use of every opportunity to help your peer supporters develop their abilities to understand other people's views and find ways forward.

Step 7: Strengths

It is important at this point in the process to remind yourself of the many and varied qualities you, your colleagues and the young people bring to this venture. It can feel overwhelming to embark upon a new and perhaps unproven project. However, try to balance an awareness of potential problems with a realistic faith in yourself and others' abilities and commitment to make a difference.

Step 8: Interventions

It is now time to describe in some detail the interventions you propose to introduce. Your proposals should follow logically from the answers in steps 1–7. If they do not, it is likely that your own preferences or preconceptions are influencing your planning. Think again about whether you are making the best use of the information gained in your needs analysis before going ahead with your plans.

Step 9: Monitoring and evaluation

At this point it is important to identify ways in which you will evaluate whether or not you are achieving your goals and ways in which you will identify unexpected changes. Now is also the time to think honestly about what you will do if your evaluation does not produce the results you had hoped for.

We have spent years talking to service managers of all types of projects who question the value of spending time on monitoring and evaluation. They often say that what little time they have, they prefer to spend on ensuring that the service is working well. However, as people who have managed small and large services with professional, paid staff and with volunteers for several years, let us put the case for ongoing monitoring and evaluation, integrated into the project from the beginning.

Why monitor?

- You cannot avoid monitoring in some form as it is essential to ensure that the peer support service, however unintrusive, is doing no harm.
- Monitoring tells you where the service is working and where it is not, information that is necessary for making improvements to the service.
- Monitoring in a systematic way takes no longer once you have set it up than monitoring in a more *ad hoc* way.
- Setting up a monitoring system from the beginning of a service allows you to tailor the system to fit the service so that it produces the information you want with as little effort as possible.
- Information gathered from systematic monitoring is particularly useful in reports to boards of governors or in funding applications.

It is important to state here that monitoring need not be formal, statistical or time-consuming. A very simple model could involve asking your peer supporters to record or remember how many young people they helped and the general nature of the issues discussed. They could then tell you this at your regular debriefing or supervision meetings and you could record the information in the table format demonstrated in Table 4.1.

Table 4.1 *Peer support service use record*

Month	Number of people seen	Types of problems
May	8	3 – peer relationships 2 – bullying 2 – family 1 – schoolwork

In addition, it will be helpful to know how people using the service evaluate it and how the service is viewed by those (the majority) who do not use it. Chapter 10 describes a range of ways of doing this.

The next step in the process is to do a needs analysis in your own work setting, using the guidelines provided in Exercise 4.1. Then in the next chapter, we will show you how to use the information you have gained through your needs analysis to set up a peer support service.

Exercise 4.1 *A Needs Analysis*

Step 1: The setting
Describe the 'culture' of your school/organization.
Questions to consider:

How are decisions made and by whom?
What is the ethos/philosophy of your organization?
How well does practice match the philosophy?

Step 2: The people
Describe the colleagues and young people (parents, if relevant) with whom you work.
Questions to consider:

What are the demographics – e.g. age, abilities, ethnicity, sexuality, etc. – of the three groups?
What are the demographic differences between the groups?

Step 3: The issues
Describe/list the problems that the young people with whom you work are facing.
Now prioritize by listing only the problems which you intend to address.
Questions to consider:

How do you know these are problems for the young people with whom you work?
Why have you chosen these specific problems to address?

Step 4: Resources
Describe the resources you have available to you in addressing these problems.

Questions to consider:

> What are the financial resources available?
> What are the material resources available?
> What are the human resources available?

Step 5: Goals

Describe the changes you want to achieve.

Questions to consider:

> Are your goals shared by
>   (a) the young people you work with?
>   (b) your colleagues?
> Are your goals SMART?

Step 6: Potential roadblocks

List/describe anything which may get in the way of achieving your goals.

Questions to consider:

> Can you do something to prevent these potential roadblocks becoming actual roadblocks?
> Even better, can you change these potential roadblocks into change facilitators?

Step 7: Strengths

List/describe the particular strengths of your organization, colleagues, young people in relation to the changes you are hoping to make.

Question to consider:

> Can you do anything to increase or make better use of these strengths?

Step 8: Interventions

Having considered all of steps 1–7 above, describe clearly the type of peer support service(s) you propose to develop.

Question to consider:

> Do your proposals follow logically from the answers to steps 1–7?

Step 9: Monitoring and evaluation

Describe the ways in which you will evaluate whether or not you are achieving your goals.

Questions to consider:

> Do you have ways of measuring unexpected changes/developments?
> What will you do if your evaluation does not produce the results you had hoped for?

5

SETTING UP A PEER SUPPORT SERVICE

In the time we have been teaching our course in peer support, we have seen many perfectly competent people successfully complete the preparation stage of planning a peer support service, the needs analysis, but founder in the second stage. It seems likely that this is more the result of anxiety about the perceived magnitude of the project, and perhaps anxiety about being judged on its success or failure, than it is about the person's actual ability to complete the task. There are two simple ways of addressing this kind of 'performance anxiety': one is to try to keep your mind focused on your original motivation for setting out on this project; and the other is to break the project down into more manageable tasks. To that end, we have divided this chapter into sections on the specific tasks that need to be completed before you can get your service up and running. There are four specific tasks to be considered in this chapter: preparation of colleagues, parents and young people; selection of peer supporters; management of the service; and administration. The fifth and more complex task of training the peer supporters is discussed in detail in Chapters 6 and 7.

Preparation of colleagues, parents and young people

It is essential to have the full backing of your management team or school governors and it helps to have substantial support for the idea from colleagues. The success of the programme is dependent on the back-up of administration in providing rooms and resources in which the peer support activity can take place. Training, advertising, producing information, circulating letters, all depend on the co-operation and acknowledgement of management and staff. Management should be consulted and given an action plan, including: a description of the programme and its aims and objectives; a list of benefits to the school, the staff and the parents; an outline of training, the model used, the trainers involved and the costs. At this point it is a good idea to arrange to explain the concept to all relevant colleagues, perhaps at a staff meeting.

Before the staff meeting, prepare colleagues by giving them some written information about the aims and objectives of the proposed system.

It will also help to have some printed information about peer support systems that have been launched successfully in other organizations. When the programme is discussed with staff, benefits and limitations should be addressed. Before the meeting, try to consider possible conflicts, such as students needing to miss class to attend training sessions, and design strategies to overcome these conflicts. Colleagues can be invited to participate to increase 'ownership' of the service by the staff. It is important to generate enthusiasm for the programme since, without your colleagues' support, it will be hard to get the service running.

Depending upon the remit of your organization, you may also want to involve parents. You may wish to provide information on the proposed service in newsletters and at parents' evenings.

The idea of developing a peer support service should be presented to the young people in a way that generates enthusiasm. Give them information about the types of peer support services used in other settings. If possible, have peer supporters from another setting give a presentation to demonstrate the work they do. Information about selection procedures can be given at this point.

Selection of peer supporters

Having the 'right' people for the job is important to any service. However, knowing who the 'right' people are and how to find them is not a simple matter. A sensitive approach and a transparent process with clearly stated criteria for selection are most likely to result in people feeling fairly treated, and can usually avoid causing unnecessary upset and offence. In this section, we will discuss methods of selection, basis for selection, choosing not to select, and some important 'rules' of selection.

Methods of selection

There are three commonly used methods of selection, each of which has distinct advantages and disadvantages. They are:

- recruiting volunteers;
- peer nomination;
- adult/teacher nomination.

Recruiting volunteers
This is a commonly used method of selection in which the whole group of young people is given some information about peer support and then asked to nominate themselves if they are interested. The most significant advantage of this method is that it empowers the young people to choose for themselves and to take responsibility for what will be their service, thereby modelling one of the basic tenets of the peer support approach. It

also is the method most likely to result in a group of young people who are truly interested in being peer supporters and thus may have a lower attrition rate than other selection methods. In addition, it allows young people to put themselves forward who may not be popular or extrovert but may possess the qualities needed in peer support. The problems that most often result from this mode of selection are as follows:

- Far more volunteers come forward than can actually be trained.
- Some of the volunteers will not be considered suitable to be peer supporters by the adults managing the service.
- Under-representation of young people from some ethnic, religious, sexual orientation and gender groupings.

Peer nomination

This method of selection involves asking all of the young people to nominate and vote for those of their peers who they think would make good peer supporters. Selection in this case is based entirely upon number of votes. Clearly, this system shares with the volunteer method the advantage of empowering the young people to begin taking responsibility for their own service. In addition, it is likely to result in high levels of credibility both for the individual peer supporters and for the service as a whole. People chosen by their peer group are likely to make peer supporters whom others feel able to confide in and thus the service is more likely to be used and useful. One possible disadvantage is that people may be chosen more because they are popular than because they have the qualities needed to be a good peer supporter. It is also less likely that youths of minority cultures (ethnic, religious, sexuality) will be nominated or voted in by the majority culture. It is also possible that some of those voted in will not really be interested in the role but feel pressured into participating.

Adult/teacher nomination

In this method of selection, the staff of the organization or school, or just those responsible for the peer support service, select young people who, they think demonstrate the qualities needed in peer support. Clearly the main advantage of this method is that the adults retain more control of the peer supporters, and, thereby, the service. Given that they are ultimately responsible for the service, this may be an attractive prospect. However, whatever this method gains in control, it loses in credibility. It will be much harder for peer supporters chosen by this method to be accepted by their peers, and, of course, there is no guarantee that the adults involved are actually any better at choosing people with the appropriate qualities than are the young people themselves. Having said this, we know of some secondary school-based peer support services that use prefects as their peer supporters with some success. Nevertheless, it seems likely that a whole group of young people, quite possibly those who most need help, will choose not to access a service run by a school elite.

If by now you are convinced that there is no ideal way to select peer supporters, then that is exactly so. The skill lies in choosing the method which best meets the particular needs of your setting, bearing in mind the relative advantages and disadvantages of the methods. The methods are not, of course, mutually exclusive. It is possible, for example, to allow peers to select from a list of volunteers or a list of young people nominated by adults. One school invited students to apply in writing and then staff selected on the basis of applications and interviews. A possible application form for this process is presented in Box 5.1.

Basis for selection

The basis for selection is closely linked to the method of selection – what you do with one influences what you do with the other. Most important is whether selection is to be based on either peers' or adults' previous knowledge and experience of individuals or whether it is to be based on the individual's demonstrated ability to perform some specific peer support skills. Selection based on prior information is open to bias, based on how well the individual is liked and/or how much the individual conforms to the selector's values (for example, perhaps a good student in the case of a teacher or a popular student in the case of a peer). In the latter alternative, often a selection day involving some training and practice in basic peer support skills is organized for anyone who is interested to attend. Selection then takes place based on some combination of self, peer and adult evaluation of the individual's behaviour and performance on that day. This method has the advantage of selection being on the more neutral and more relevant basis of the individual's actual ability to demonstrate some of the skills and attitudes needed in the role of peer supporter. In addition, our experience is that very often individuals who are considered by others as unsuitable to be peer supporters come to this conclusion for themselves following a day of peer support exercises, and subsequently de-select themselves. Thus this method has the supreme advantage of increasing individuals' self-awareness whilst doing no harm to pride or status within the group. It may appear a method that takes up too much time or is too costly (if you have someone from outside helping with the training). However, our experience is that it costs less time to select properly in the beginning than it does to deal with the problems arising from inadequate selection as the service is implemented.

It is probably evident by now that we support a method of selection which empowers young people to make their own choices and take responsibility for their service from the beginning, but which helps them make this choice from an informed position – informed about their own strengths and weaknesses and how those relate to the requirements of the role of peer supporter.

Box 5.1 *Peer support application form*

Name:

Form Teacher:

Peer support will use some of your free time, for example, one lunch hour per week. What are your other commitments?

How will you deal with any conflict in time?

Do you ever talk over your problems with your friends?

Why do you think that you would be a good peer supporter?

What experiences have you had that would help you to be a peer supporter?

Please complete and return to Ms. X by 1st October

I give permission for my son/daughter to be involved in the peer support initiative at school.

Signed:................................... (parent or guardian) Date:...............

Exactly which qualities and characteristics your peer supporters will need depends to some degree on the type of peer support service you plan to have. If you are planning a peer education service in which older adolescents facilitate groups of younger adolescents, for example, then you may choose peer supporters who have a reasonable level of social confidence and who are articulate. If, however, you plan a face-to-face, counselling-based service, then you may prefer peer supporters who are good listeners and naturally discreet. You will also need to decide whether to select solely on the basis of the individual's interpersonal skills or whether to take into account a young person's previous experience of coping with difficulties, or indeed his/her own need for involvement in a peer support project as an aid to increasing self-esteem. The general 'rule' about using people who have experienced serious problems themselves is 'Do not use them while they are still struggling with the problem but do use them once they have come through it.' In fact, some of the best peer supporters are likely to be young people who have had to develop coping and survival strategies themselves. This is clearly demonstrated in a number of youth drug projects where young ex-users act as peer educators and counsellors to other young people. Most peer support projects also include some peer supporters who are there more for the benefits in terms of social inclusion and increased self-esteem that participation can give them than for the contribution they can make to the service. A well-managed and well-monitored service should have no problem accommodating a few such participants. In fact, it is very important that peer supporters learn from the beginning that it is possible to both offer help and need help. Otherwise there can be an unhealthy and unhelpful tendency for those in the supporting role to deny their own problems and over-focus on those of others.

Choosing not to select

Those people who decide not to select but to take on everyone who volunteers usually do so out of a judgement that this practice best models the principle of empowerment that is at the basis of peer support. If this is your choice, you need to plan carefully what you will do with people (and there will certainly be some) who do not seem appropriate for the role but who still wish to participate in the peer support service. The most practical and positive solution is to have a system of peer support which offers a range of different roles designed to make the best use of different individual strengths. In this system, the school bully who happens to draw well can design posters to advertise the service. The real strength of this approach is its recognition and valuing of individual difference. It also allows for an individual to develop into someone who can be relied on to listen and to help with problems, and this can be signified by 'promoting' them to a new role within the peer support service.

A few important 'rules' about selection

There are some rules that should be adhered to if at all possible:

- Ensure that your group of peer supporters reflects the characteristics of the population they will support – in terms of ethnicity, religion, gender, sexuality, and so on.
- Begin as you mean to go on. If you intend to retain a fair degree of control over the service, then use a method of selection that gives you a similar degree of control. If you intend to place most of the responsibility with the peer supporters, then use a method that gives them responsibility from the beginning.
- Choose a method of selection that is as empowering of the young people as you can manage. This will be different for different people and settings, but remember that all aspects of setting up and managing a peer support service should model an attitude of respect and a belief in the ability of young people to be a part of their own solution.
- Use a process of selection which is open and fair and as inclusive as possible. Ideally, create a process that helps unsuitable people to de-select themselves. However, if someone is completely unsuitable, don't be afraid to turn him or her down, but be prepared to provide an honest and sensitive explanation of your reasons.
- On a practical note, ensure that you select sufficient numbers to cover the attrition that always occurs as people experience the reality of being a peer supporter.

Management of a peer support service

In our experience, most successful peer support services have one person who is responsible overall and who is actively involved in the running of the service. If you are that person:

- **Be involved in the initial training of the peer supporters.**
Some people feel anxious or too inexperienced in the necessary skills to run an experiential training and decide to 'buy in' someone such as a counsellor. We cannot stress strongly enough that this is unlikely to be helpful in the longer run. Counsellors may be able to practise counselling skills, but this does not mean that they can teach them or adapt them to suit peer supporters, or that they know much at all about peer support. Instead, consider some other options such as: deciding to set up a less counselling-based type of peer support service for which you already have the skills to train supporters, getting some training yourself and then challenging yourself to train the peer supporters; or if you do want to 'buy in' someone with counselling experience, then co-facilitate the training with them. Some advantages of this option are that you will have the

opportunity to learn the necessary peer support skills, you will be able to provide the input which ensures that the peer supporters are trained for the roles they will be taking on rather than in counselling skills in general, and you will get to know your group of peer supporters, with their strengths and weaknesses as a group and as individuals. If you still feel unable to train your peer supporters yourself, then, at the very least, ensure that you attend all of the training with them. The training is perhaps the most important time for the development of a group identity and cohesion that will be important to its successful functioning later on.

- **Be the person (or one of the people) who provide(s) regular debriefing/ supervision.**

The need for regular debriefing or supervision is discussed in detail in Chapter 9. In terms of management of the service, the important point is that you need to be in a position to hear from your peer supporters about what they are doing, any problems they have encountered, and any further learning needs they have. This is another area in which some people who feel perfectly able to manage and set up a peer support service feel insufficiently trained and experienced. Again the temptation is to 'buy in' someone, usually a counsellor or psychologist who has training and experience in counselling supervision. This can be problematic as people external to the service may not be sufficiently familiar with the requirements and limitations of peer support and of your service in particular, and they may keep information confidential between themselves and the peer supporters, thus leaving you, as the service manager, without important information about problems arising. The best solution is probably either to ensure that the service you manage is not beyond your capacity to supervise, or to get an external person with supervision experience to co-facilitate debriefing/supervision groups with you so that you can develop the necessary skills. If, against our advice, you do decide not to involve yourself in supervision, then make sure you build into the external supervisor's contract that s/he must disclose to you important issues arising in the debriefing/supervision, and arrange regular meetings with her/him to review the progress of individual peer supporters and the service in general.

- **Be responsible for ensuring that the goals of the service are clear, and for monitoring whether and to what degree they are being met.**

You are in the best position to do this. You may, of course, actively involve the peer supporters in agreeing the goals of the service and in collecting and recording information regarding uptake.

- **Have a system of ongoing review leading to any developments/ changes needed to the peer support system.**

In our experience, reviewing a service can be a time-consuming and apparently mindless exercise imposed from above (for example, to obtain ongoing funding/support) or it can be a fascinating and creative look at where the service is doing well and where and how it needs to change. Do your best to make it the latter by relating it specifically to the original goals of the project and using it as an opportunity for the peer supporters to use and develop other skills: for example, group facilitation skills to collect ideas and information from the group; information technology skills to collate and report the information; public speaking and/or drama skills to present it at a school assembly or conference.

- **Be the main point of contact for any problems associated with the service, whether the concerns of peer supporters or complaints about the service.**

However unpleasant it may be to hear negative comments about a service you have put energy and commitment into, it will be far better to hear about them directly and in time to correct them than indirectly and too late to do anything about them. For this reason it is important that you create an atmosphere which allows peer supporters, other young people, staff and parents to talk to you about any concerns they may have about the service, in the knowledge that you will listen attentively and then take appropriate action. Many problems are made worse by waiting, so encourage your peer supporters to tell you about their concerns as soon as they can. The best way to sustain equanimity in the face of criticism of a service you are committed to is to hold in mind the truth that, however good a job you and others do, you will all make mistakes from time to time. Your job is to predict and prevent those problems you can, and deal honestly and efficiently with those that you haven't managed to predict or prevent. Whilst you don't want to make a peer support service a very complicated entity, do have a process of investigating complaints before taking action on them. It can be an extremely helpful learning process for young people (in fact, for any of us) to make a mistake, have it fairly and helpfully dealt with and to learn from it.

- **Have the energy and faith to sustain the project when the peer supporters (and perhaps your colleagues) lose theirs.**

We choose our words advisedly when we write 'when' rather than 'if' regarding loss of faith in the project. This is because our experience and the experience of the people who participate in our courses is that there is almost always a point when the service is ready and the peer supporters are keen to do the work they have been trained for, but there is hardly anyone using the service. This can be very discouraging and often makes the peer supporters and others question the value of their service. It is also a time when some of the less committed peer supporters may drop out. As the manager of the service, you will need to retain your belief in the service based on the understanding that it takes time for young people to try out the peer supporters and to trust that they can be helpful and that the service really is confidential. This may be the time for an assembly or information session to remind the other young people of the existence of the service, or it may be the time to think again about any possible reasons why the service is not being accessed.

- **Have a management team to support and advise you.**

We do know people who have done all the planning, setting up, training, managing and supervising of the peer supporters by themselves. They are easily recognizable by their grey hair, lined faces and high sickness levels! Unless you have a very small-scale, uncomplicated buddying or befriending service, it is hard work to do everything on your own. You are unlikely to have all the skills you need, and if you are doing it in addition to your regular job, as many of you will be, it is likely to take up most or all of your lunch hours and after-school time and possibly some weekend time as well. So one reason to have a team or at least one other person to support and advise you is to have someone to share even a small amount of the work. The second reason is to help you keep up your faith in the service when all about you are losing theirs (as mentioned above, this will happen from time to time). The third is that you should have someone who can help you monitor the service objectively. If you have put time and energy into developing a service, it can be hard to see or admit to any weaknesses. But the ability to do this, to make changes and to carry on is often the differentiating factor between services that work and those which fade away. It is often a good idea to ask someone else from within your organization and someone from outside who can contribute skills which complement your own. For example, sometimes someone from the school psychological services or community mental health services may be interested in this type of project as it falls under the wide heading of 'preventive mental health'.

If this section makes managing a peer support service sound like an onerous task, then there is probably some truth in that. However, it is important to keep in mind the positive effects the service may have on the peer supporters themselves, on the young people using the service, and on the atmosphere in the school or organization where it is running, to say nothing of your own learning and development. People and places with whom we are in contact who have a successful peer support service consider it well worth the time and effort involved.

Administration

Good administration makes every service more efficient and effective. For this reason, it is important to plan from the beginning what your peer support service will require in the way of administrative procedures and practices. The exact needs will be different for different types of services in different settings, but all will have some administrative needs. Our suggestion would be to aim for administrative procedures which are clear, simple and the minimum necessary to meet the needs of the service. The following are some suggested areas of administration you will need to consider.

Marketing

In their questionnaire survey of 54 peer support services in secondary schools and colleges, Naylor and Cowie (1998) found that 'promotion and publicity' of the service were seen as essential in increasing levels of use by young people. Peer supporters themselves will probably have ideas of how best to market their new service. The most usual ways are through direct contact, such as speaking at a school assembly or to individual class groups, or at other gatherings which young people regularly attend, and through development and distribution of written material such as posters and leaflets. It may be that a subgroup with particular talents in this area is given the responsibility for marketing, or all peer supporters may be involved in different ways, depending upon their skills. In the first case, it is a way of involving some of those young people who are interested but who are not yet ready to do peer support work. In the second case, the activities of developing publicity material and presentations can be used to establish group identity and cohesion, both factors which will positively effect the sustainability of the peer support service in the long term. It is important that some publicity be targeted at staff as well, as they are in a good position to encourage young people to use the service and their support is vital. Finally, remember that marketing is not something that just happens when the service is beginning. Most of the services we know have had periods when their use has declined, often due to a decline in awareness of the service. Peer supporters need to take every opportunity to raise or maintain the profile of peer support in their school or organization so that they continue to feel involved and people continue to use the service.

Accessibility

A peer support service needs to be as accessible as possible. At a minimum, this means that potential users need to know how and when to contact a peer supporter, and the process for doing this needs to be one which does not draw attention unnecessarily to the person needing support. Many services do have a room 'staffed' by peer supporters at specific times where anyone can drop in if they want to talk. However, for some young people this will be too exposing. In Naylor and Cowie's (1998) study, some services increased uptake simply by encouraging peer supporters to offer their help 'whenever and wherever' it was sought. It may also be helpful to post a list of which peer supporters will be available at which times, as some young people will feel more able to talk to a particular peer supporter or a peer supporter of a particular gender or ethnic group. On the whole, professionalization mitigates against accessibility. Therefore, where problems of low uptake are experienced or anticipated, it may be best to plan a form of peer support that takes the service to the people rather than expect the people to come to the service!

Record-keeping

Usually when record-keeping is mentioned during our training courses, a groan goes around the room. It is true that most people who decide to set up a peer support service already have more than enough paperwork to keep them occupied. For this reason and reasons of user confidentiality, aim to keep only as much recorded information as you definitely need. Unless there is a good reason for it, do not ask peer supporters to keep records that could identify the young people using the service. Many services will not require any records apart from a brief note made by the service manager after debriefing sessions about the amount and content of work done. Even for more complicated, counselling-based services, it will usually be enough to have a record of some demographic data (for example, age-group, gender, perhaps ethnicity), the reason for seeking help, the name of the peer supporter and the number of times the person was seen. This is sufficient information to give a picture of the amount and nature of the work being done. In the case of someone presenting with a reportable problem such as sexual abuse of a minor, the peer supporter should be required to discuss this with their service manager/supervisor immediately and any responsibility for recording information can then be taken by the manager/supervisor. Any records that are kept should be anonymized and have limited access. The best practice is one in which only the service manager/supervisor has access to all of the records, with peer supporters being allowed access only to the records of the individuals they personally support. There should be no need for staff uninvolved in the peer support service to have any access whatsoever to the records of individual young people. Good practice and procedures for ensuring confidentiality are addressed in detail in Chapter 8.

Supervision/debriefing

As we have found the provision of regular supervision or debriefing to be one of the main factors influencing the success of a peer support service, the content and process of providing supervision and debriefing are detailed in Chapter 9. However, some of the issues which you will need to consider when setting up the service are: how often you will meet with the peer supporters; whether they will be required or invited to attend; whether you will see them individually or as a group; the type and degree of information you will want from them; and where you will meet them. In addition, you will need to make provision for peer supporters to contact you if they are faced with an urgent situation such as a young person who seeks their help being in immediate danger.

Referral

A peer support service is able to help young people with quite a range of problems, but it is not designed to offer professional help or to deal with problems which seriously threaten their well-being. Therefore, it will certainly be necessary at times to refer a young person on to a professional with particular expertise in the problem area. It is important to develop a local referral network before your peer support service begins. This will involve both obtaining the telephone numbers of important local services and speaking to someone directly about the peer support service and agreeing a process for making referrals, including urgent referrals where necessary. Having a personal contact with a service almost always results in a faster and more successful referral, so don't be tempted to skimp on this aspect of preparation. Minimally, you should know how to make an urgent referral to local authority duty social work services and psychiatric assessment services. In addition, you may well need to refer to the school psychology service, youth counselling services, youth sexual health and pregnancy advisory services, specialist eating disorder clinics, youth drug and alcohol services, or a local bereavement service. One way of making a doubly useful contact with these services is to ask them to come and speak to the peer supporters on their specialist subject as a part of the ongoing peer support training programme. There is nothing to be lost by asking and they may well be interested in the concept of a peer-run service that addresses some of the psychological and social issues faced by the young people they see professionally.

Service monitoring and review

We have already presented the case for setting up a service in which a process of ongoing monitoring and review is integrated from the beginning rather than 'tacked on' when a report to some external funding or governing body is needed. Therefore, it is only necessary to emphasize here that the process should be meaningful to the peer supporters – that is, they should see the relevance of the information collected – and it should be simple to administer.

Exercise 5.1 will help you plan and develop a peer support service based on the findings in your needs analysis. Once your planning is complete, you will be ready to move on to Chapter 6 for a detailed look at training peer supporters.

Exercise 5.1 *Developing a peer support service based on a needs analysis*

Having completed your needs analysis, we suggest you plan your next
steps in a systematic way. On our trainings, participants do this exercise
in groups so that they can benefit from the ideas, experiences and
constructive criticisms of others. If you are planning a peer support
service on your own, try to co-opt another person from your school/
organization who would be willing to help you see any gaps there may
be in your thinking. This plan will certainly not be the final product, but it
should serve as a basis from which to begin setting up your peer support
service.

Based upon the findings from your needs analysis, answer the following:

1. Is peer support a suitable option to meet the needs you have identified?
    Is it the best option or one chosen out of necessity?

2. Which model(s) of peer support do you think will best meet the
    identified needs and why?

3. List the next steps in implementing the development of a peer support
    service with a provisional date for completion of each step.

4. **Selection**
    How will you select peer supporters?
    Do you envisage any difficulties in this – e.g. finding suitable volunteers,
    deciding who is suitable, turning down unsuitable volunteers?
    How many will you select/recruit and why?

5. **Training**
    Who will do the training of the peer supporters?
    When, where and in what format will it be?
    Are there any difficulties envisaged in offering this training – e.g. trainers'
    lack of skill/experience in particular areas – and how do you propose to
    overcome them?

6. **Management**
    Who will manage the service?
    Will this conflict with other roles/responsibilities, and if so how will the
    conflict be managed?

7. **Administration**
    Discuss how you plan to organize the following aspects of administration
    for the service you are developing:

- marketing;
- access;
- record-keeping;
- supervision;
- external referral;
- service monitoring and review.

PART III

TRAINING IN PEER SUPPORT

6

CORE SKILLS FOR PEER SUPPORT

People using this book will have varying levels of experience in peer support skills and in teaching. Often on our trainings, there are two distinct groups of people – those who have much experience of using counselling and or group work skills but little teaching experience, and those who have little experience of counselling skills but who are trained and experienced teachers. Each group brings its own strengths and usually has its own learning to do.

In order to aid those different types of learning, this chapter is divided into a section on process – that is, how to teach peer support skills – and another section on content – that is, what to teach. The process section explains the particular style of teaching we recommend for peer support skills and offers some research findings as to the effectiveness of these teaching methods. The content section covers the basic attitudes and core skills of peer support and gives some examples of exercises to use when teaching them to young people.

There are, of course different skills needed for different types of peer support services. These next two chapters on training are designed to be used as a guide to help you think about the specific training needs of your peer supporters rather than to be used in any prescriptive way. The section on process is likely to apply to all levels of training in peer support, but the actual skills you choose to teach may vary with the type of peer support service you are offering.

Process

In this section, we will look at some of the key issues involved in training peer supporters using experiential teaching methods.

What is experiential learning?

Experiential learning is often described as learning by doing. In fact, doing is only one aspect, though an essential one, of the experiential learning process. In order to ensure a true integration of the skills being taught, it is important to guide learners through the complete process of experiential learning which involves:

- having an active experience and/or observing others having that experience;
- reflecting on the experience;
- drawing some understandings/general conclusions from the experience;
- attempting the activity again with the benefit of new understandings gained.

Adapted from Kolb (1976)

One of the most important ways of enhancing learning in the experiential learning model is to strengthen the links between the active experience and the reflective activity that follows it. Some of the ways this can be achieved in the context of peer support are described later in this chapter and in the debriefing sections of the sample exercises provided.

Why experiential learning?

Research findings suggest that experiential learning is particularly effective for exploring and changing attitudes and for developing interpersonal skills, precisely the type of learning which peer supporters need (for example, Jaques, 1984; Weil and McGill, 1989).

Experiential learning has particular benefits in training peer supporters. First, it is accessible to a wide range of young people and may be particularly appealing to young people who have not been successful in traditional educational settings. When done well, it requires everyone to participate, but allows and values different styles of participation, from the quiet young person who listens well, to the extrovert young person who can speak openly about his/her feelings, to the physically confident young person who finds the solution to a spatial group exercise. Second, it addresses learning at many different levels – practical, emotional, social and cognitive – with the result that learning is more easily retained and replicated in 'the real world'. Equally important is the fact that it can be tremendous fun. Our experience is that when people are having fun, they can concentrate for longer and they are more willing to take risks. Thus they learn more and feel more able to put the learning into practice.

Are there any disadvantages to experiential learning?

In our view, all of the potential disadvantages to experiential learning can be avoided if it is done well. For some people, the experiential style of teaching may be unfamiliar, and for others there may be the memory of negative personal experiences as a result of this teaching method. Either of these can create anxiety and even resistance at the thought of using these teaching methods. To help people overcome this anxiety and because it is the style of teaching we recommend using for peer supporters, we use this method of training ourselves on all of our trainings for managers and trainers of peer supporters. For those of you who must work through your anxieties on your own, we will attempt to address some of the issues which often arise in our trainings.

Lack of control

It is usual for trainers to feel anxious about 'everything' getting out of control when they use experiential exercises. The best way to avoid this is generally to give clear instructions, with clear time-limits on exercises and a clear signal to indicate the time when everyone should listen for your next instruction. It is also important to be flexible. There is no rule that certain exercises should take certain lengths of time. So, if the group is engaged in the exercise and learning from it, there is no reason not to give them more time to finish it off. It is also important to walk around the room and keep an eye and ear on what is happening. In this way, if something is getting out of hand, you can intervene early. Finally, it is worth accepting that occasionally an exercise may get out of control and you may have to intervene. Depending upon how much insight you think the group has and how much strength you've got at the time, you can either suggest that the group look at what happened and the implications of this for them being peer supporters, or you can simply move on to another, more contained activity. Over many years of training young people, we have not encountered a serious problem of control. One of us has, however, had to resort to using a whistle as the signal to gain the groups' attention and to explaining and supervising exercises with her hands on the shoulders of rowdy participants!

The exercise 'doesn't work'

Usually by this people mean that the young people either do not follow instructions or they do not appear to learn the skills the exercise is intended to teach. Most often this is as a result of the exercise not being well explained or supervised or debriefed. However, remember the need for flexibility. If it doesn't work, then move on to something that does. Afterwards, give some thought to ways you can adapt it next time so that it does work. Also, in any training, you will probably need several attempts at teaching some skills before everyone grasps them, so don't expect too much from only one exercise. Finally, in these circumstances, try to remind yourself of the psychotherapeutic concept of every experience being 'grist for the mill'. If the group is not learning what they are intended to learn, then try to think about what they might learn from the experience as it stands. For instance, if they can look at their lack of compliance, they may be able to learn something about why people don't do what they are advised to do – a useful piece of learning for a budding peer supporter.

Participants being 'too emotional'

As experiential exercises can sometimes tap emotions that the young person is not fully aware of, it is important to think before you begin about exactly how much emotion is too much in the group training situation. In general, everyone should be encouraged to be only as open as they can live with on a day-to-day basis, particularly if they have contact with each other outside the training group. We always make this point explicitly at the beginning of the training and from time to time throughout as exercises which might tap emotions or painful experiences are introduced. For the most part, this helps participants maintain a helpful level of openness. However, occasionally someone becomes angry or tearful as a result of an exercise tapping their own issues. In this situation, you may choose or you may offer the person the choice as to whether they leave the group and deal with their feelings elsewhere, or whether they stay in the group, providing an opportunity for the group to learn about helping people with difficult feelings. Group learning should not be at the expense of the individual, but it is possible for it to be a learning and supporting experience for all parties. It is, of course, important not to exceed your own capacity for working effectively with emotional situations in the group.

Teasing/bullying/conflict in the group

We have noticed over the years that even with a contained, well-taught peer support training, there is often a point at which some kind of conflict or bullying occurs in the group. At first, our reaction was to stop it immediately, pointing out the inappropriateness of peer supporters behaving in this way. However, over time, we have come to a different understanding of this behaviour, with the result that we have chosen to take a different route through it. Our current understanding is that one way or another, bullying and conflict are significant issues for many people who choose to become peer supporters. At some level, they know they need help in addressing these issues if they are going to be good peer supporters, and one way of getting this help is to act out the problem in the group.

Therefore, when some incident of teasing or bullying happens now, as it usually does, we explicitly welcome it and offer it to the individuals involved and to the group as an opportunity to learn in 'real life' about an important issue in peer support. This kind of 'real-life' learning is something that has an impact no amount of teaching could. It is also invaluable in demonstrating how a potentially difficult situation can be worked with to come to a positive or 'win–win' solution.

In fact, the two ways of dealing with bullying in the group are not mutually exclusive. Even after the experiential work we have suggested, it is important to reiterate the limits of acceptable behaviour within the training group so that it is not a recurring problem.

Perhaps the main point to draw out from this section is that while there can be difficulties in using an experiential teaching method, the advantages far outweigh the disadvantages. The key is to have the courage to try it and accept that it will not always work as you had planned. At times, you will achieve some surprising results as Example 6.1 illustrates.

Example 6.1

In the context of what can go wrong in experiential trainings, we always think of training we facilitated where anyone who was interested was allowed to attend. The result was that many young people attended who had some interest in peer support but rather more in missing their classes. One young man spent most of the day literally swinging from the rafters in the training room, taking part only to disrupt the experiential exercises. At the end of the day, we asked all of the young people to share something they had learned during the training, and, to our surprise, this young man offered one of the most insightful comments about himself in relation to the training that we had heard in a long time. So a lesson we now remember is that learning often takes place, despite all evidence to the contrary!

Key issues in experiential teaching

There are a few points of practice which will make your experiential teaching more likely to succeed.

Model attitudes and behaviours
It is important to model in your training the kind of attitudes and behaviours you want the peer supporters to adopt. This involves being more conscious than usual to be, for example, respectful, non-judgemental, willing to admit to mistakes, and boundaried. This type of behaviour is effective both in that it demonstrates what you are trying to explain and

also in that it creates a relaxed and open learning environment. In addition to modelling, it can help to be explicit about your attitudes to learning. Make it clear that you want people to take risks and that making mistakes is fine as these may be different values from those they experience daily in school or work.

Agree ground rules

It is essential to set ground rules about attitudes and behaviour with the group before beginning the training. Most groups can tell you the rules they think are important, and you can list them so that they can be referred to later if needed. Basic ground rules should include: respecting the views and beliefs of others; confidentiality within the group or small group in which the discussion takes place; listening and not speaking over others; participating in the exercises. Leave out this step at your peril!

Give clear instructions

It takes a surprising amount of skill and preparation to give instructions for experiential exercises clearly so that someone who has never before seen the exercise can carry it out successfully. Until you are experienced in experiential training, we would recommend writing your instructions down and then reading them out in a step-by-step fashion to ensure that you do not leave out a vital piece of information.

Debrief exercises

One of the reasons experiential teaching is sometimes not as effective as it should be is because the exercises are not debriefed. In this context, debriefing means taking a few minutes at the end of each exercise to emphasize the main points the young people need to learn from the exercise. This can be done either by asking them what they learned from the exercise or by having a bullet-point list of the relevant learning outcomes.

Provide opportunities for practice

Trainee peer supporters will only integrate these attitudes and skills if they have opportunities to practise them from different angles. For example, they can do the same exercise once being the peer supporter and then again being the 'client' or person being supported. Have exercises which allow them to review what they have learned, to demonstrate to the group, to offer and receive constructive criticism so that if they don't get it from one angle, they get it from another.

Create a supportive atmosphere

We all meet the needs of others better if our own needs are being met. Therefore, a successful peer support training also addresses the need of the helpers. Try to create an atmosphere in which people can admit to problems and concerns so that they can be helped either to use their own experiences positively or to keep them separate from their role as peer supporter.

Have fun
Do present the exercises in a way that allows the young people to have fun and laugh at themselves. Some of the exercises are quite exposing, some of the skills are difficult to master and some of the topics that arise may be hard for people to deal with. Therefore, what usually works best is a balanced approach combining serious discussion with more entertaining but still useful activities to put some of the ideas into practice.

As a final comment on process it is perhaps worth emphasizing our view that how you teach something is at least as important as what you teach. Most of the problems that arise during trainings are due to lack of attention to process rather than lack of knowledge of content. Therefore, give enough time and energy to getting your group of peer supporters ready to learn and working well together and you can be fairly sure that the training will be a success.

Content

This section will describe the core attitudes and skills needed by most peer supporters and will give some examples of exercises that can be used to teach and practise those skills. We have taken the ideas for some of these exercises from Trevor Cole's Canadian publication *Kids Helping Kids* (1987). He trained with us on a number of peer support trainings and kindly agreed that we could use our variations on his exercises in this book. Some others are exercises that have simply been around the counselling and personal development circuit for so long that it is not possible to identify their original source. The exercises in Chapters 8 and 9 are entirely our own inventions. You will probably find that this process of modifying well-known exercises or developing new ones to meet your particular needs becomes a part of your training repertoire as you gain experience. Meanwhile, we hope that the exercises in this book, which have been used in many peer support trainings, will prove helpful to you.

How do I choose what to teach?

The answer may be obvious, but in case it is not, what you teach needs to be related directly to the attitudes and skills your peer supporters will need to have in the particular type of peer support service you are developing. Peer supporters in a buddying or befriending service, for example, will benefit from training in peer support qualities and attitudes, but may need only a limited range of peer support skills. To aid you in your choice, this section describes the purpose of the exercise, the procedure, and then the issues to cover in the debriefing to ensure that the young people you are training are getting the most they can out of the exercise.

Peer support qualities and attitudes

Regardless of the particular type of peer support service, most peer supporters need to have similar qualities and attitudes. This section of training exercises aims both to bring out those qualities and attitudes already present in the peer supporters and to help them develop those they are lacking. Some of the specific qualities and attitudes we are aiming for are: ability to work co-operatively; interest in others; inclusiveness; valuing difference; openness and fairness. Box 6.1 is a list of the qualities that young people have identified as being important to them when they are talking about a problem to a peer supporter.

Every part of the training can work towards reinforcing these qualities where they exist and developing them where they do not. Therefore, our work in this area begins with introductory exercises, then moves on to co-operation exercises, and finally finishes with an activity which moves the training from general attitudes to those more specific to peer support.

Box 6.1 *The qualities of a good peer supporter*

- trustworthy
- doesn't judge you
- listens and doesn't tell you what to do
- friendly and approachable
- won't tell anyone what you have told him, even if you are fighting and he could use it against you
- kind
- honest but not critical

Introductory exercises
Exercises 6.1, 6.2 and 6.3 are three examples of the many possible exercises used to begin training sessions as a positive note.

Co-operation exercises
'Changing places' – (Exercise 6.4), 'Knots' (Exercise 6.5) and 'Angels on the head of a pin' (Exercise 6.6) are some examples of exercises which we use to help young people (and adults as well!) work together and think about the advantages of co-operation. In addition, these are all active exercises and so serve to liven the group up when that is needed.

Exercise 6.1 *The name game*

Purpose
To get to know everyone's names and to begin to interact positively and purposefully with other members of the group.
An additional benefit is often that people begin to help others out when they can't remember and the process of valuing individuals' different strengths, so crucial to group cohesion, begins.
The purpose of the trainer going last is to begin to model that taking risks will be valued and that it is all right to make mistakes.

Procedure
One person begins by saying their name. The person beside them then has to say the first person's name and their own. The third person says the first and second persons' names and then their own. This goes on until everyone has said their own name and all of the others preceding them. One of us usually places herself last so that she has the most difficult task.

Debriefing
This exercise does not need debriefing but we sometimes simply point out that some people found it easier than others and that others will find other exercises easier and that this mixture of skills is exactly what is needed in a good peer support service.

Exercise 6.2 *Introduce your neighbour*

Purpose
To begin to feel more comfortable in the group by interacting purposefully with one member.
To discover your own level of skill in questioning someone else and in talking about yourself.
To get everyone speaking in the large group, even those who would normally avoid it.

Procedure
Give the group five questions they need to ask their partner (the person sitting next to them). They should be factual questions but they can also be amusing or unusual. They should not be very personal or revealing.
Each person has a short time (3–5 minutes) to do this in. Then they must come back to the large group and each person must introduce their partner to the group based on the information they have gathered.

Debriefing
Without pointing out individuals, it is worth noting that some people seem to have listened well and remembered the information given to them whilst

others did not. If you discuss it in the group, you will probably find that some people took up more than their share of time talking. This can be pointed out without judgement by saying that one of the things you hope each person will learn is which skills they need to work on.

Exercise 6.3 *Getting to know you*

Purpose
To get to know people's names.
To interact purposefully with several group members individually.
To practise asking questions of people you don't know.
To begin to notice similarities and differences between yourself and others in the group.

Procedure
Give out a sheet of questions (see sample) with blanks to fill in with group members' names.
Give the group something like 15 minutes to walk around the room and find someone who meets each criterion. Do not stop until all the blanks are filled in.

Debriefing
There are three possible ways of debriefing this exercise. One is to ask people to talk about the experience of asking questions of people they do not know well. Related to this one might ask the question: 'Now that you know this information about the person, do you feel you know them?' with the intention of leading on to how knowing facts is less useful than knowing how someone feels. The other is to focus on unexpected similarities and differences discovered in the interaction and how they might influence people's feelings about each other or about being in the group.

Getting To Know You!

This activity will help you gain more information about people in this peer support training. Walk around and find someone who matches each description.

    1._____ wears the same size shoe as me.

    2._____ was born in a foreign country.

    3._____ has a birthday in the same month as me.

    4._____ has a brother.

5._____ is someone who does a sport regularly.

6._____ is good at maths.

7._____ speaks at least three languages.

8._____ knows how to cook.

9._____ has a pet cat or dog.

10._____ lives in a flat.

Exercise 6.4 *Changing places*

Purpose
To create a positive atmosphere within the group.
To highlight similarities and differences in the group.
To raise energy levels in the group.

Procedure
Get the group to sit in a circle all facing into the centre. One person then
volunteers to stand in the middle and that person's chair is removed. This
should leave one chair fewer than the number of people.
The person in the middle then says: 'I like everyone in this group but I
particularly like people *wearing green*'. At this everyone who is wearing green
has to get up and quickly find an empty chair to sit in. One person will be
left without a chair and s/he will then become the speaker. The italicized
phrase should be changed each time to include colours, clothes being worn,
hair and eye colour and other non-intrusive pieces of information. (We
emphasize 'non-intrusive' after our work with groups of young offenders in
which the questioning included the previous night's sexual activity, unusual
sexual practices and current drug use!)

Debriefing
Probably the main points to raise from this exercise are:
1. How any of us can influence the atmosphere in a situation, in this case
just by the use of the positive phrase: 'I like everyone.'
Sometimes to highlight the point and have some fun, we imagine the
atmosphere that would have been created if we had been saying: 'I am going
to kill everyone unless they are wearing green!'
2. How there are always lots of similarities and differences amongst people
in groups whether we know it or not, and this will be true of people being
supported also.

Exercise 6.5 *Knots*

Purpose
To encourage co-operation and demonstrate the effects of lack of co-operation.
To demonstrate the different responses of individuals to a problem and the strengths and weaknesses of each approach.
To energize the group.

Procedure
This activity can be done in groups of 5–20. Larger groups become unwieldy.
To form the knot, everyone stands in a circle, shoulder-to-shoulder, and places their hands in the centre. Everyone then needs to take two hands of two different people, neither of whom should be their immediate neighbour on either side.
The task is to disengage the knot without letting go of hands.
Pivoting on the handholds is allowed and so is going over and under arms whilst still holding hands. If completely stuck, one letting go is allowed.
The group should find themselves in one large circle or occasionally two interconnected ones. No time-limit is set for this activity.

Debriefing
In the process of disengaging the knot, some people, 'activists', will quickly rush in going over and under other members' arms attempting a solution by chance.
Others, the 'analysts' will favour a more considered approach in which one or two people take responsibility for guiding others' movements. Since all members are in the knot together, at some point the group will need to decide which approach they want to follow. The process by which this occurs can be revealing about individuals' roles in the group.
Debriefing should include taking feedback from the group regarding the effects of co-operation or lack of it and the advantages and disadvantages of different styles of problem-solving

Exercise 6.6 *Angels on the head of a pin*

Purpose
To encourage co-operation and demonstrate the effects of lack of co-operation.
To demonstrate different responses of individuals to a problem and the strengths and weaknesses of each approach.
To energize the group.

Procedure
Divide the class into groups of 8–10. Give each group a piece of wood or stiff cardboard about 12 inches by 12 inches (30cm × 30cm).

The task is for the group to plan a method for all members of the group to be supported off the floor by the wood/cardboard at the same time for a period of 5–10 seconds. Five minutes is allowed for planning, but no rehearsal is allowed.

When the time is up, ask each group to show you its solution.

A variation on this activity is to ask the group to try to execute their plan without talking.

Debriefing

As with the 'knots' exercise, debriefing should focus on how the group came to the solution rather than the actual solution reached.

Debriefing should include taking feedback from the group regarding the effects of co-operation or lack of it and the advantages and disadvantages of different styles of problem-solving.

In addition, this exercise, unlike 'knots', has the potential for finding a creative and 'original' solution and thus can illustrate the particular advantage of co-operation in finding a solution that no individual could have come to on their own. The group can be asked to relate these findings to peer support.

Quality-identifying exercise

Exercise 6.7 is one which links the introductory and co-operation exercises with the peer support skills training which is to come. It helps the young people focus on the qualities they will need if they are to be good peer supporters.

Exercise 6.7 *Think of a secret*

Purpose

To identify the qualities of a good peer supporter.

To provide the opportunity to recognize that the young people on the training already possess many of these qualities.

Procedure

Ask each person in the group to think of a secret that they have never told anyone and/or something they would find it very difficult to talk about. *Emphasize that they will not be asked to reveal this secret at any time in the exercise.*

Then ask them to look around the group and think about which person in the group they would tell their secret to if they had to tell one person. *Ask them not to reveal who this person is.*

Now ask them to think about what it is about that person that made them choose him/her.

Debriefing

Take feedback from the group by asking them to call out the attributes of the people they have chosen.

Write this in a list that can be seen by the group and kept for future reference.

When the list is complete, ask the group to provide a title. Usually they will see that it should be called something like: 'The Qualities of a Peer Supporter'.

Finally, draw the group's attention to the fact that they already had these qualities within the group. This sets the group up on the positive note that they have skills to learn but that they already possess some of the basic qualities needed.

Core peer support skills

The core peer support skills are certain to be needed in any peer support service that has a counselling basis. In addition, they will be useful for young people involved in befriending or in peer education. In fact, they are probably useful skills for any young person to learn, as they form the basis of good interpersonal communication. Repeated practice will be needed in order that your peer supporters master the skills sufficiently to use them when they are actually in a peer support situation. Having said that, it is not realistic to aim for perfection. Those of us with years of counselling and psychotherapy experience do not get it right all the time! All that is necessary is that peer supporters learn enough about good communication from these exercises to be able to be of some help to their peers.

The skills that we consider to be core skills are: giving feedback, attending, listening, responding, questioning and waiting in silence. As in the previous section on qualities and attitudes, we will discuss each in turn and then offer examples of experiential exercises to use in teaching them.

Giving feedback

As most of these exercises involve learning based on feedback from peers, it is important to spend a little time at the beginning talking about ways to give helpful but not uncritical feedback. Usually we ask the group for suggestions and then draw up a list of guidelines for feedback. These guidelines are then placed conspicuously at subsequent training sessions so that they can be referred back to if anyone becomes unhelpfully critical of others. The list usually looks something like the one in Box 6.2.

Attending

Attending means, very simply, behaving in a way which indicates that you are interested in the other person – in short, paying attention to them. We usually begin by asking the group to name some of the behaviours that

Box 6.2 *Giving feedback*

Consider the following when giving feedback on others' work in exercises:

- Wherever possible, give both positive and negative feedback. If you give the positive first, the person is more likely to listen to the negative as well.

- Comment on the person's behaviour rather than the person.

- Offer your feedback as a possibility or a question, rather than as a statement of fact. For example: 'I was wondering if . . . ' rather than 'You should have . . . ' or 'I'd have done it this way . . . '.

- Do not avoid negative comments, but try to be constructive in your criticism.

- Listening to feedback and trying to improve is important in developing your peer support skills. However, giving helpful feedback is just as important a peer support skill to develop.

---

indicate that someone is willing to pay attention to you, and then list these on the board. Next we offer them an acronym to remind themselves of the main points. One such from Cole (1987) is **FELOR**, which stands for:

Face the person you are listening to
Eye contact
Lean slightly towards the person
Open posture (rather than closed)
Relaxed rather than rigid posture.

Another similar acronym is Gerald Egan's (1994) **SOLER**, which stands for:

S: Face the client **squarely**, i.e. adopt a positive stance that indicates involvement.
O: Adopt an **open** posture. The 'open' can be taken literally or metaphorically. Crossed arms and legs can be interpreted as a sign of lesser involvement. The important thing is to give the message: 'I am open to you right now.'
L: **Lean** towards the other. A slight inclination towards the other person is a sign that you are interested in what that person has to say.
E: Maintain good **eye contact**. Keeping steady, direct eye contact with another person shows that you are intent on what they are saying. It

does not mean that you have to stare at the person and it does allow for glancing away from time to time.

R: Try to be **relaxed** and natural in your behaviour and not to use anxious or nervous body language. (adapted from Egan, 1994, pp. 91–2)

Whichever you choose to use, they should be useful reminders rather than absolute requirements. There is no need for a specific exercise to illustrate these points. Much fun and learning can be had simply by asking various group members or the whole group to illustrate open versus closed postures, and so on. You can also ask people to work with a partner to discover which is a comfortable distance to sit apart, how much eye contact is comfortable, how closely they should lean, and so on. In general, asking people to illustrate the 'wrong' way of doing it is more fun and is just as useful for learning, as long as you finish off with an illustration of the 'right' way.

Exercise 6.8 is one that links attending to listening and is fun and quick to do.

Exercise 6.8 *Roadblocks to communication*

Purpose
To illustrate the importance of attending by providing the opportunity to feel what it is like not to be attended to.
To illustrate the importance of listening by providing the opportunity to feel what it is like not to be listened to.

Procedure
Ask people to get into pairs and sit on their chairs facing each other.
Ask one person to take the role of the person needing help and one the helper. Ask the person needing help to think of a problem (nothing serious) they could talk about. Give the helper a card with instructions on how to behave and ask them to do exactly what the card says. Two of our favourite behaviour cards are included, but you can make up your own.

Debriefing
After just two or three minutes, stop the action and bring the group back together. Feedback should be taken first from the 'client' as to how it felt to be ignored or talked over. This exercise usually provokes strong feelings of anger or not being valued, in addition to much laughter. Then take feedback from the 'helpers' regarding how it felt to behave in this unhelpful way. We usually conclude with a question to the group about what they think we want them to take from this exercise. The conclusion need not be complex or sophisticated, but it is important to summarize in order to ensure that everyone has got the point you intended and remembers it when they are using their peer support skills in a real situation.

Behaviour cards

> When your partner starts to talk, look at the floor or off into the distance, shift in your seat, clean your nails, generally looked bored. Do not offer any response that encourages the person to carry on talking, just say, 'Yeah, yeah' in a bored way.

> As soon as your partner has described their dilemma, interrupt, talking over them if necessary to given advice. Tell them how you would handle the situation. Don't leave much space for your partner to talk about their experience. Say something like: 'You think that's bad, you should hear what happened to me!'

Listening

Good listening is one of the most difficult skills to teach. For the purposes of peer support, we tend to break it down into two components: listening for content and listening for intent.

LISTENING FOR CONTENT   This involves learning to listen accurately for relevant information. It is important to help young people realize that we are all inclined to put our own interpretation on stories and to help them find ways of setting these aside and listening as closely as possible for the 'client's' view of his/her problem and situation. Exercise 6.9 is designed to help young people focus on accurate listening.

Exercise 6.9 What did s/he say?

Purpose
To learn to listen accurately to a story and to relay it accurately to another. To begin learning to give critical but helpful feedback to a peer.

Procedure
Divide the large group into smaller groups of three.
Depending upon your preference and the creative abilities of the group, either give each person a story or have them make one up.
Each story should have sufficient detail that it takes about 5 minutes to tell. The teller needs to be able to remember the detail to test for accuracy later.
Ask the teller (person 1) to tell person 2 the story while person 3 *does not* listen.

Then have person 2 tell the story to person 3 in the presence of person 1 whose story it is. At this point, person 1 can correct any errors person 2 is making in the telling of his/her story.

The group can do this three times to give everyone a turn at telling and listening.

Debriefing

In the large group, ask people not to comment specifically on their own or others' mistakes, but to talk about the difficulties they had in listening and remembering accurately. Discuss the factors that made it easier or harder to listen and draw conclusions for their work as peer supporters. An example may be that the noise in the room was distracting, and this will help your peer supporters remember the need for a quiet, private place to talk when they are supporting someone.

Also focus on how it felt to give and receive critical feedback and use this to get the peer supporters to begin to think about ways of helping people see something that is difficult for them.

LISTENING FOR INTENT   Having mastered (to some degree, at least) the idea of listening accurately, peer supporters then need to learn how to listen selectively. This may involve identifying particular aspects of the story or perhaps 'hearing' what is behind what is being said. These are quite complicated skills so we would recommend teaching them only to the degree that your peer supporters will need to use them.

To simplify matters, peer supporters can be taught to select on two main bases: one is feelings and the other is importance. In the first case, it is considered a supportive action to help people identify and express their feelings about a problem. Therefore, peer supporters can be helped to pick up on expressed or hinted-at feelings. In the second case, peer supporters can help by identifying the most salient issues from the 'client's' story which can be helpful in finding a solution to the problem later on.

Exercises which can help with the development of these skills are variations on Exercise 6.9. The simplest way to practise is for the trainer to develop some storylines with guidelines as to how the individual is feeling about their situation. Either in small groups of three or four or in the large group, a young person is then asked to role-play that person and to tell their story. The group is asked to identify how the person is feeling and what the important points are from their story. This can be followed by discussion of how this information might be used to help the person feel better or resolve their problem. All of these exercises should be fairly brief and address issues relevant to the young people involved in order to keep the group engaged. Example 6.2 is one possible storyline (one which comes from a young person one of us spoke to), but do make up your own to suit your peer supporters' circumstances.

Example 6.2 Family problems

Well, I came to talk to you because I don't know what to do. Since my Dad left, my Mum has been working a lot, sometimes a double shift just to make ends meet. If she works a double, she leaves at 6 a.m. and doesn't get back until 11 p.m. That means that my older sister and I have to cook for our younger brother and sister and make sure they bathe and go to bed. That was working all right for a while but now my sister has started going out at night and not coming back until just before our Mum gets home. Mum doesn't know and she'd kill her if she found out. She's out with a gang of girls who hang around with some boys who deal in drugs. I don't know if she's using drugs or not because she won't talk to me about it. She just says I can't tell Mum or she'll get in trouble. Now I don't have any time to do my school-work and I'm getting in trouble with the teachers. I really want to get my exams so that I can get a decent job. There is no one I can talk to because I don't want to get my Mum or sister in trouble, but I can't go on like this either.

There can never be too much listening practice. The training skill is to keep the group interested by developing storylines or involving them in developing storylines which directly address the issues they are likely to encounter in their own lives and the lives of the peers they support.

Responding
There are many possible skills of responding that can be taught to peer supporters. However, it is important not to make this more complicated than is absolutely necessary for the peer support role your young people are going to fulfil. The responding skills outlined below are useful in most peer support roles, and, as with the listening skills, useful in communication in life in general!

NOT GIVING ADVICE   If we could only say one thing to a group of new peer supporters about responding, we would say: *'Do not give advice.'* We all have a tendency to want to give someone who is upset a solution to their problem. It makes us feel that we have been helpful. Therefore, the tendency in newly trained peer supporters is for them to listen to the person's story and then jump in with: 'If I were you I would. . . . ' As this seems a helpful action on the surface, you will need to talk with the group about why it is unlikely to be helpful in the long run. We usually do this in a discussion format and then list some points to remember on the flip-chart as illustrated in Box 6.3.

Of course, you cannot ask young people not to give advice without offering them some ideas of what to do instead. There are two basic answers to this point. One is that many peer supporters help simply by being available to listen and there is not necessarily a need to find answers.

Box 6.3 *Why a peer supporter should not give advice*

- Your solution may not be another person's solution. Just because something has worked for you in your situation does not mean it will work for someone else in their situation. There may be something you don't know about which prevents it from being helpful.

- If your idea doesn't work, they may lose faith in you and in the peer support service in general.

- If your idea causes even more problems (this can happen if you don't fully understand the other person's situation), they may blame you.

The second is that if they want to try to help more actively, then they need to learn a way of helping people find their own answers. A fairly simple way of doing this, called 'Five steps to problem-solving', is covered in Chapter 7.

In our experience, trainee peer supporters almost always ask what to say if someone asks them directly for advice. As this is a skill that many trained counsellors have difficulty learning, we tend to offer some specific sentences/phrases which they can use in response to a question such as the one in Exercise 6.10.

Exercise 6.10 *What do you think I should do?*

Purpose
To provide an opportunity to practise responding to a direct request for advice.

Procedure
In pairs, have one person ask the question, 'What do *you* think I should do?' and the other person try to respond with one of the following phrases or something similar.

- Well, I don't know your situation as well as you do, so why don't we look at it together and see if we can come up with some ideas.
- I can't tell you what to do, but I want to try to help you find an answer for yourself.
- I can't give you advice, but I can help you look for your own answer.
- Well, from what you've said so far, it sounds like you could do x, y or z. Why don't we talk about those ideas and see which one is most likely to work.

Debriefing
Ask peer supporters to discuss how it felt not to give a direct answer and
how it felt not to receive one.
Ask the peer supporters to identify what the common emphasis is in these
answers and why it is better to use them than to give a direct answer.
The emphasis in these answers, as you can see, is on finding a solution
together rather than giving advice, and it is towards this that peer
supporters should be aiming.

Exercise 6.11 is a simple exercise which we use to help peer supporters
practise the skill of not giving advice. It is one of a range of exercises which
follow the three-person role-play model in which one person is the person
with a problem, another is the peer supporter trying to help them, and the
third is the observer who will offer constructive criticism of the peer
supporter's skills after the role-play has finished.

Exercise 6.11 *To advise or not to advise*

Purpose
To provide an opportunity to practise responding to a direct request for
advice.
To begin to practise helping someone without advising them.

Procedure
Divide the group into smaller groups of three and assign or ask for volunteers to the three roles for a role-play.
Give the person needing help a role card with a storyline including a
problem on it. It should take only a few minutes for them to tell their story
to the peer supporter. Instruct them to ask the peer supporter directly
what s/he thinks they should do about their problem once they have told
their story. If the peer supporter avoids the question, suggest that they ask
it again more forcefully.
The peer supporter should not be told the exact purpose of the exercise.
Instruct the peer supporter simply to do what they can to help the person
with the problem.
Tell the observer the purpose of the exercise and ask them to record or
remember exactly what the peer supporter does and says in response to
this question.

Debriefing
When the role-play is over, the observer should give feedback to the peer
supporter regarding how they responded and the effect of that response on
the person needing help.
In the large group there can be further discussion of how best to respond to
the pressure of someone wanting advice.

Suggested scenarios for the role cards

My friends are avoiding me and are going around the school saying I'm a slut. It's because a boy one of them has fancied for a long time asked me out and I went out with him. I didn't say anything, but he told his friends and now they've told mine and it's all over the school. I like this boy but I don't want to lose my friends. What do you think I should do?

I'm really worried about my brother. I know he's hanging around with a gang who use hard drugs and I guess he's using too. Everyone knows the gang deals and I think he's going to get into serious trouble. He always comes in late and sleeps through school. My parents shout at him but I don't think they know what he's doing. I don't know what to do. What do you think I should do?

There are three boys who keep taking my lunch money. They wait at the bus stop and as soon as I get off they take it. When I say 'no', they threaten me and say they're going to beat me up or cut me. I know one of them sometimes carries a knife so I'm afraid and I just give it to them. I don't want to tell on them in case they find out and get me anyway. What do you think I should do?

A FEW WORDS OF ADVICE ABOUT THE USE OF ROLE CARDS   Whilst we have given you some suggestions from our own experience, you can increase your repertoire of stories by drawing on your own experience and that of your peer supporters. Problems they encounter are more meaningful to them and result in greater engagement than any we could suggest. Once you get into practice, the scenarios come readily to mind and need only be written up in brief. We usually give people the bare bones of the story and suggest that they elaborate on it as they see fit. This makes the role-play more realistic as they introduce elements of their own issues and lives. Do, however, ensure that the basic point of the exercise is understood by the 'client' and the observer so that they can keep the exercise 'on track' despite any elaborations!

It is equally possible to use this method with groups of people who do not read well or are not all literate in the same language. It is just as easy to brief the 'clients' and observers verbally as in writing.

FOCUS ON FEELINGS We have already mentioned the counselling assumption that helping people identify and express their feelings is likely to make them feel less alone and more able to find a way forward. Based on this assumption, we teach young people to guess from someone's expression, body language and verbal cues what they are feeling and then to frame a response based on that information.

One quick and simple way to work on identification of feelings is to sit in a circle and have one person at a time quickly demonstrate a feeling through facial expression and body language and have the group guess what it is. The other alternative is for you to shout out a feeling and have everyone in the group demonstrate it.

Responses should be kept as simple and to the point as possible. They should also be exploratory rather than didactic. This is true of responses on any issue and the phrases suggested in Box 6.4 could be used to respond to many comments. Their common element is that they help identify the feeling, problem or issues without forcing the peer supporter's interpretation of the situation onto the 'client'.

Exercise 6.12 is an easy way to practise this skill.

Box 6.4 *Helpful responses*

- It sounds as if (you're feeling) . . .
- It seems like (you're feeling) . . .
- I wonder if (you're feeling) . . .
- Am I right in thinking that (you're feeling) . . . ?
- Does that make you feel . . . ?

Exercise 6.12 *What do you say after you say 'hello'?*

Purpose
To practise helping someone identify and express their feelings.

Procedure
Put a list of possible phrases (see Box 6.4 for suggestions) on an overhead or flip-chart for the group to refer to.
Start the group off with a statement such as: *'I can't ever seem to get my maths right. I just can't understand it and the teacher never has time to help.'*
If you want to have some fun and defuse some of the embarrassment young people often feel at using studied responses, you can always start by asking the group to provide some unhelpful responses. In our experience they do this with more creativity and energy than when providing helpful responses! An example would be: *'Everyone can do that maths. You must be really stupid!'*
Then ask the group to give some appropriate responses that address the feelings behind what is being said. An appropriate response would address

the 'client' feeling discouraged with his/her inability to understand and/or anger with the teacher for not helping.

Peer supporters can either use some of the suggested phrases or come up with some of their own, bearing in mind the goal of responding in an exploratory rather than intrusive way.

Ask group members to come up with their own sentences for the group to respond to. This part of this exercise encourages the peer supporters to think about the different ways feelings can be expressed and helps in identification of feelings.

Debriefing

Debriefing in this case simply involves summarizing the characteristics of unhelpful and helpful responses. Try to remember always to end with the material you want the young people to remember.

Questioning

As always, whether or not training in this skill is necessary for your peer supporters will depend upon the role they will take. For those who will use some listening/counselling-based approach, there are two main aspects of questioning that are important to learn: asking questions for a purpose and asking questions in a way that helps the client.

ASKING QUESTIONS FOR A PURPOSE   Our experience is that anxious beginning peer supporters (and indeed beginning counsellors) have a tendency to bombard the person seeking help with questions, particularly of a factual nature. In this case, the purpose of the questioning is usually to make the peer supporter feel in control and that s/he is doing something useful. It rarely serves to help the person needing help. It is important, therefore, that peer supporters be taught to ask questions only if they are likely to be helpful to the person seeking help. Questions should not be asked to fill a silence or because the peer supporter doesn't know what else to do. Example 6.3 illustrates this.

Example 6.3

A 16-year-old girl is talking to a peer supporter about what a difficult time she has had since her mother died of cancer a year ago. The inexperienced peer supporter may not know what to say and consequently may seek information such as the exact date of her mother's death or where her funeral was held. This usually has the effect of making the 'client' feel she has not been heard or understood, as the date of her mother's death or the location of the funeral is not the issue at all for her. However, a more experienced peer supporter might ask the girl simply to tell her more about how she has been feeling or coping since her mother's death, which is much more to the point.

Peer supporters can practise asking questions for a purpose in the three-person role-play format. The best scenarios to practise this are ones in which the person seeking help has either a serious or embarrassing problem or s/he is very emotional. Assign a story and emotional reaction to the 'client' and then ask the person playing the peer supporter to do whatever s/he thinks is most helpful. The observer can note whether the peer supporter asks too many irrelevant questions and then the group can discuss what prompted the peer supporter to do so and what s/he might have done instead.

ASKING QUESTIONS IN A WAY THAT HELPS THE 'CLIENT' It is also useful for peer supporters to learn how to ask questions which help their 'client' express him/herself . The simplest way to do this is to explain the difference between closed and open questioning and to encourage peer supporters to develop the ability to ask open questions. Working definitions of the two concepts follow:

Closed Questioning: This involves asking questions which can easily be answered with a 'yes' or 'no', or which force a specific answer, or which assume an understanding of the meaning an experience has for the person seeking help. Some examples of closed questions would be:
'Do you get along with your parents?'
'Do you like school?'
'Do you feel angry about what the bully did to you?'

Open Questioning: This encourages the person to explore and elaborate and makes no assumptions about the meaning of the experience or the feelings evoked. Some examples of open questions would be:
'How do you get along with your parents?'
'How do you find school?'
'How do you feel about what the bully did to you?'

Most people seem to be more familiar with asking closed questions. Therefore, it takes practice to learn to ask open questions and sometime to see the value of open over closed questions. Exercise 6.13 is one which young people usually enjoy for its novelty value!

Exercise 6.13 *Teacher (or group leader etc.) on the spot*

Purpose
To learn the value of open over closed questioning.
To practise formulating open questions.

Procedure

Ask someone who is usually in authority over the young people (e.g. teacher, headteacher, group leader, peer support trainer) to be 'on the spot' and sit in the middle of a circle formed by the group of young people.

They need to be willing to answer (not necessarily honestly) questions asked of them by the young people. *You* need to be prepared to divert any particularly intrusive questions.

Brief them to answer all closed questions with a yes/no or as uninformatively as possible but to give an informative answer to any open questions.

Then ask the young people to shout out, one at a time, any questions they have always wanted to ask this adult.

Once a question has been answered, ask the group whether it was open or closed and what kind of response it received.

After a few minutes of a variety of questioning styles, put the list of openings on an overhead or flip-chart and suggest that the young people try using it to ask open questions of the teacher.

Debriefing

Ask the group to summarize from their current experience the advantages of using open questioning for the person needing help and for the peer supporter.

Further practice will be needed and is probably best done in the three-person role-play format where the person playing peer supporter can try to ask open questions and the observer and 'client' can give feedback on whether or not it worked and how it felt.

Examples of Open-Ended Questions

What does that feel like?

Can you tell me more about . . . ?

Would you like to talk about . . . ?

Where would you like to begin?

How do you feel about . . . ?

Can you tell me what that means to you?

How would you like things to be?

What have you thought of?

What would you like to do about . . . ?

What's that like?

What can you think of?

What's most important for you now?

Waiting in silence
Sometimes the most useful action any listener can take is simply to sit quietly and attentively and wait to see what the speaker says next. However, this is also one of the most difficult skills for anyone, adult or young person, to learn. At the very least, it is important to give peer supporters permission to wait and think before they speak rather than saying the first thing that comes into their head just to fill the silence. We are not suggesting that a peer supporter sit in silence for a long period of time, as this is more likely to make the 'client' and the peer supporter anxious than it is to be helpful. However, a minute or two's thinking- and feeling-time should be encouraged.

When you come to practise 'waiting in silence' with your peer supporters, you will find that many cannot do it. At first, most people laugh, speak or fidget. However, practice, while not making perfect, does make for improvement in this skill. It is usually best to practise this skill in a graded way that allows the young people gradually to overcome their discomfort. (See Exercises 6.14 and 6.15).

Exercise 6.14 *Staying with silence*

Purpose
To develop an increasing ability to sit with someone without speaking.
To develop an understanding of how it can be supportive not to speak immediately.
To develop strategies for helping peer supporters wait in silence.

Procedure
Start by asking your peer support trainees to choose a partner and then to sit facing that person without speaking or fidgeting for three minutes.
Then ask the group for feedback on how it felt to sit in silence.
Gradually increase the young people's tolerance by increasing the length of time, asking them to sit with someone they do not know well, looking at the person they are sitting with, etc.

Debriefing
Each time, ask for feedback on how the experience felt and what ways people found to help themselves to sit quietly.
It can be useful to draw up a list of suggestions to assist peer supporters, such as a phrase they can repeat in their head to help themselves remain calm – e.g. *'I'm just going to sit here quietly and think about John'* or *'It's alright not to say anything for a few minutes.'*

Exercise 6.15 *Think before you speak*

Purpose
To practise waiting and thinking before responding to someone needing help.
To understand why it can be helpful to think before speaking.

Procedure
Using the three-person role-play format, give the 'client' a problem to talk about (use role cards or just problems that come to mind).
Ask the peer supporter simply to try not to 'jump' into responding immediately, but to wait for a moment before speaking.
Ask the observer to comment on whether this worked.
Ask the 'client' to give the peer supporter feedback on the effect this had on her/him. As always, it is at least as important that the young people be able to reflect on the process as it is for them to 'get it right' first time.
This exercise can be made gradually harder by introducing increasingly difficult situations such as ones in which the 'client' is very emotional or is asking for advice.

Debriefing
Most role-play exercises are best debriefed by asking the group to tell you what they discovered in the exercise. You can then summarize the points that you want them to take away. In this case it would be that although waiting can make the peer supporter anxious, sometimes it is more helpful because in the silence either the 'client' elaborates and the peer supporter understands the situation better or the peer supporter has time to think and is more likely to say something helpful.

The final stage at this level of training is to integrate all of the skills we have covered in this chapter. The simplest way to do this is to practise being a peer supporter using the three-person role-play model described earlier and ensuring that each peer supporter has a chance to try out all three roles – peer supporter, person needing help, observer. Exercise 6.16 gives some suggested scenarios to practise with. However, you can also make up your own to suit the problems your peer supporters are likely to encounter.

If the peer supporters you are working with can master most of the skills described in this chapter, they will already be skilled enough to deal with a wide range of problems. For further development, Chapter 7 details training in more complex and more specialized areas of peer support.

Exercise 6.16 *Role-play scenarios*

You have recently joined a new school. You started halfway through term and everyone had already made their friends. You feel very lonely. Your accent is slightly different from the other students and whenever you try to make friends with anyone, they tease you about the way you speak. Now you are frightened to talk to anyone in case they make fun of you.

You normally hang around with two other friends. You have known one of them since you were at primary school. Recently, both of them have been ignoring you deliberately and leaving you out. Yesterday, you found out that they have been telling the rest of the class all sorts of terrible stories about you. Some of the things they have said are true and are things you trusted your friend to keep secret.

This is the sixth school you have attended and you are now in Year 9. Your father died suddenly when you were 7 years old, and, soon after, your mother had a 'nervous breakdown' and was in hospital for a long time. Since that time, you and your sister were looked after by relatives and then lived in three different foster homes. Your sister does better in school than you and seems to adjust to the changes. You never feel that you belong and always feel bad about yourself. Recently, you have started cutting yourself, first with a pen and then with a razor. They are just small cuts where no one can see them, so no one knows you are doing this. While this makes you feel better at the time, you know it is probably not good for you and you are worried that you might be 'mad' like your mother.

Recently, your mother and father have been arguing a lot, although they used to get along well. You have heard your mother threatening to throw your father out of the house. Last week, your mother talked to you and told you that your father has been having an affair with a woman at his work for the last three years. Your mother found out quite recently and has told your father that he must end the relationship or leave. You feel caught in the middle because you love your father and don't want him to leave, but you also understand your mother's feelings. You feel you should do something to help, but you don't know what.

Two students in your class keep asking you to give them money. They have told you that if you don't give it to them by next Friday, they will beat you up. They are known to be tough and you have heard rumours that they carry knives.

You are 16 and you have been involved with a boy, your first real boyfriend, for about a year. You think you love him and he loves you, but you both have plans to go to college and so you don't really want to settle down with him. You have recently started having intercourse, and the first few times you didn't use any protection. You are now on the Pill, but your period is a month late and you are very worried that you might be pregnant. Your mother is always warning you not to 'bring your problems home' and so you don't feel you can talk to her.

You have always been 'a bit chubby', but now that you are at secondary school, it really bothers you. All of your friends are wearing stylish clothes and talk about how 'fat' they are. You know that you are fatter than them but they try not to say it because they like you. Recently, you have started vomiting after eating and you are quite pleased as you have lost weight. But you are also worried because you know it isn't good for you and yet you can't stop.

7

FURTHER SKILLS FOR PEER SUPPORT

In this chapter, we focus on specific information and skills which are needed to provide the more complex forms of peer support – those that we have broadly defined as counselling-based approaches. In the first section, 'Five steps to problem-solving', we build on the core skills introduced in Chapter 6. We outline more specific ways of helping a person to resolve a problem, by (a) identifying the problem, (b) exploring options, (c) identifying risks and benefits, (d) making an action plan, and (e) evaluating the results. In the second section, 'Developing empathy', we describe ways of training peer supporters to deal more effectively with difficult feelings. In the third section, 'Conflict resolution', we look at the nature of conflict and indicate ways in which peer supporters can be trained to deal with it constructively. Some of the exercises involve personal disclosure/exposure. The facilitator must be sensitive to the potential impact of these activities on young people who see one another regularly. It is important to remind participants not to raise issues that may embarrass them later. If in any doubt, use already-prepared vignettes or role-plays.

Five steps to problem-solving

We recommend that you get into the habit of structuring the helping process into five steps. The five exercises in this section (Exercises 7.1–7.5) give opportunities to practise the work of guiding the person through the five steps towards action that contributes to a resolution of the problem in a way that is appropriate and feasible.

The first step involves identifying the problem. This is not as easy as it sounds since often the person with a problem is so immersed in it that they are not able to describe it coherently. If the person is to be helped, however, an essential step in the process is to be able to state what the problem actually is. If possible, the problem should be described in concrete, specific terms, preferably in the present tense and without assigning blame or sympathy to either party. It is a good idea to encourage the 'client' to 'own' the problem.

The second step concerns the process of exploring options and beginning to consider goals that the person seeking help would like to achieve. It is useful at this stage to enable the person to list forces that prevent them from attaining their goal as well as forces that might enable them to achieve it. They can also be encouraged to list the forces that are strongest at present, whether positive or negative, and discuss action steps that could strengthen the facilitating forces and weaken the restraining forces. This process will lead naturally to stating a list of action steps that might enhance the facilitating forces, whatever these are.

The third step concerns choice that takes account of risks and benefits to the person seeking help as they begin to select the means to attaining their goals. It is important to choose actions that are in line with the person's own values and that are feasible within their particular context. The risks must be faced. It is also helpful to try if possible to help them to select actions that are likely to meet with some success, but also to support them if the desired goal is not attained immediately.

The fourth step involves making a plan of action. At this point, if the person is ready, it is helpful to prepare them for possible outcomes, including failure, success or the unexpected. They should also be given a time and place to meet again to report back on the action and to reflect with the peer supporter on its effectiveness in attaining the goal.

The fifth step is about evaluation. Here the peer supporters looks at their own behaviour, how others responded, whether the problem was resolved and to what extent, and how they feel about the action plan. It is possible that the action uncovered new problems or new perspectives on the issue. At this point of evaluation, new strategies may emerge or it may be necessary to start the problem-solving cycle again.

Developing empathy

An essential component of attending to another person as they tell the story that currently preoccupies them at that point in time is the capacity to have empathy for that person's situation. This means that, to be an effective peer supporter, you must develop an understanding of that person's situation as they themselves experience it. Of course, we can never totally enter into the world of another person. But there are ways of building on the intuitive ability to take the perspective of another that, we hope, will have been identified during the earlier exercises.

Egan (1994: 106) argues that the helper enters the world of the other person 'through attending, observing, listening and "being with" deeply enough to make a difference'. From this perspective, empathy is a way of coming to understand the client's view. It is also important *to let the client know* that you understand. The quality of empathy involves cognitive understanding and emotional sensitivity. The process of putting some of these thoughts and feelings into words helps both the peer supporter and the user of the service to clarify what the issue is. By exploring these feelings, a context is created for moving towards a deeper understanding of the problem and of the options open to the person.

In training, peer supporters need to be given varied opportunities to practise the skill of attending with empathy to the other person. Exercises 7.6–7.9 are helpful in this regard.

Conflict resolution

> There is nothing insipid about being a peacemaker in a war game, whether within a family or a youth club or between nations. Conflicts release overwhelming personal energies and it is a brave person who has the guts to step in when the situation is ablaze. (Fine and Macbeth, 1992a, p. 5)

Conflict is unavoidable and occurs in most settings at some point – at work, at school, in organizations and in the community. Conflict is a part of life for all of us. We cannot alter that fact. However, we can have an influence on how conflict is managed and how we respond to it.

There are four basic ways of responding to conflict:

- **Fight:** Generally, when people use physical or verbal responses to conflict, we have a competition. This is known as a 'win–lose' situation, and results in one person using power to win over the other person.
- **Avoidance:** This occurs when either one or both parties avoid the situation. They either will not admit that there is a conflict or they refuse to deal with it. This results in a 'lose–lose' situation.
- **Compromise:** This occurs when both parties bargain, so that each side gets something they want, but also has to give up part of what they want. This still becomes a 'lose–lose' situation.
- **Problem-solving:** This is called the 'win–win' approach. When this approach is used, both parties agree to work on the problem and find a solution that will meet the needs of both sides.

In this way, both parties will get almost all of what they both want. In this section, we recommend Exercise 7.10 and 7.11.

It is essential in training to emphasize that conflict resolution can be viewed as something daring and exciting. It is not bland to be a peace-maker. Rather it is a challenging activity that results in greater social accomplishment and gives the mediator a deeper understanding of inter-personal relationships. The process of confronting conflict can be made an empowering experience rather than an act of violence. Throughout their inspiring books, Fine and Macbeth (1992a and b) use the image of fire to illustrate the different ways in which people can respond to the conflicts that are, as they indicate, potentially in all communities or relationships. They demonstrate how there are contrasting ways of dealing with the 'fuel' that is the raw material of the 'fire' that can escalate when there is a conflict. The people involved can allow tensions and disagreements to smoulder or they can look for areas of shared concern to respond to the fire. Once the smouldering fuel begins to burn, they can either agitate the situation further or demonstrate growing support for those who are making a constructive, shared response to the issue. Once the fuel begins to burn, the people involved can either allow it to escalate through prejudice, disaffection and poor communication or they can make a collective response with the possibility of achievement of a shared goal for all. From the first type of response comes damage to all involved, while from the second comes inspiration, achievement and a sense of collective pride in resolving a difficult issue. Exercises 7.12 and 7.13 enable participants to explore this process.

The literature on conflict resolution often treats negotiation between two parties without an intervening third party as different from conflict resolution in the presence of a mediator. However, as Björkqvist and Fry (1997, p. 251) suggest, the division is somewhat arbitrary since the same psychological elements are required in each process. For a successful negotiation to take place, the parties involved need to take account of the other's point of view as well as their own. Where there is no mediator, this can be considered as an 'internalized third-party perspective'. The exercises throughout the present book provide the opportunity to train peer supporters to adopt this reflective stance on their own conflicts and issues. In the particular context of conflict resolution, the training enables them to facilitate mutual perspective-taking between parties in conflict who are unable to communicate effectively without the presence of a mediator. In other words, one of the aims of the peer supporter should be to enable those seeking help to develop their own internal third party.

In offering training in mediation and conflict resolution, peer supporters need to build on the listening and facilitating skills already described in Chapters 6 and 7, and add to these a step-by-step process that assists two or more people who are in conflict to agree a mutually acceptable solution. There are six basic steps:

- **Defining the problem:** Each participant is given an agreed amount of time to describe their view of the problem situation, without interruptions. Feelings are heard as well as facts. The mediator clarifies the needs and interests of each party by saying, 'My understanding of what you said is this. . . . And before you tell me your view, I would like you to summarize what the other person said.' The mediator does this for each party. At the end of each account the mediator summarizes what has been said to check for accuracy and to allow both parties to hear and reflect upon this.
- **Identifying the key issues:** All issues arising from the accounts are listed on paper. They are divided into non-conflict issues and conflict-related issues. (If the literacy levels of participants are low, or if participants

have poor concentration, this step can be done verbally, in less detail but still effectively.)

- **Visualizing an ideal solution:** Both parties state ideally what they would like to see happening in the future to improve the situation.
- **Brainstorm possible solutions:** Both parties are encouraged to suggest solutions to any of the conflict issues identified earlier. They can be written down. Until now, most of the communication has been directed to the mediator. Now the conversation will become more three-way. The mediator asks each party to think about the outcomes of each solution were it to be implemented, not only for themselves but for each other and for other people.
- **Negotiation of a plan of action and agreement:** The mediator asks the participants, 'Which of these solutions will most likely meet the needs of both of you?' One or two solutions are identified. These are clarified to ensure that each party knows who will do what by when, and then a written agreement of future actions is drawn up and signed by all present. Both parties shake hands.
- **Follow-up:** A date is made to meet again in the future to evaluate the outcomes of the mediation.

This process must be practised by peer supporters in training. We have found that role-play followed by discussion and supervision is the most valuable way of learning the skills of mediation.

Exercise 7.1   *Stating the problem or central issue in concrete terms*

Purpose
To learn to listen carefully to another person's story and elicit the key features.
To practise paraphrasing skills.

Procedure
The group sits in a circle. You have prepared four or five short descriptions, in the words of the person bringing a problem to peer support, that describe the issue, the feelings around that issue, and a decision that has to be made, for example:

> Girl of 15: 'People keep spreading rumours about me. They whisper things about me behind my back and pass notes around the class about me. No-one talks to me at break anymore. I hate school so much now, though I didn't before, and wish I could leave it. I'm planning to ask my mum to take me away from school – or I might run away instead.'

One person reads out the statement, sentence by sentence, and the members of the group respond by paraphrasing what the person has said. Alternatively, a member of the group makes a statement about his or her own experience of a problem, his or her feelings and a decision to be made.

Debriefing

Ask the person who read the statement to say which paraphrased responses were most helpful and why. Focus on the nature of the issue, the feelings aroused and the action planned.

Members of the group are then invited to comment on how and why the paraphrasing was done. This exercise gives an opportunity to talk further about the difficulties the peer supporters may have in giving advice rather than listening, in missing the chance to explore feelings, and in being judgemental about proposed action plans.

In this exercise, peer supporters are given the opportunity to enable a person with a problem to explore alternatives to their current way of dealing with the issue and considering what the outcomes may be to a different plan of action.

Exercise 7.2   *Exploring alternatives and weighing up the risks*

Purpose

To learn strategies for helping the person to consider and explore alternative ways of dealing with the problem.
To address the issue of risk to the person taking action.
To practise some helpful questions.

Procedure

The group sits in a circle. You have prepared vignettes, in the words of the person bringing a problem to peer support, that describe a situation and the unpleasant feelings that have been aroused.
Examples:

'My family is moving away to another town. I am really scared and will miss my friends so much. Mum and Dad do not seem to have noticed.'
'Though I worked really hard this term, my marks in English were rock bottom. Now my teacher treats me as if I were stupid. She never asks me questions any more and yesterday told me off in front of everybody. I feel so annoyed about this and I just can't find the energy to work at English at all.'
'Everyone has been asked to Bea's birthday party except me. I have cried myself to sleep all week.'

The group decides who is to take the roles of speaker and supporter. The speaker states the problem. The supporter gives responses that invite an alternative way of looking at the problem, for example:
'What do you want to happen?'
'What could you do to make that happen?'
'As I see it, from what you have said, you have these choices.'
'Another option might be . . . '
'Let's brainstorm how you could handle this . . . '

Debriefing
Ask the person who read the statement to say which responses were most helpful and why. Focus on the risks and benefits involved in the action planned. Members of the group are then invited to discuss the responses and to develop further responses of this kind. This exercise gives an opportunity to explore ways of guiding the person with the problem to begin the process of making an action plan and to be empowered to make a judgement about the relative costs and benefits of different types of action. You can also discuss the difference between this kind of response and advice-giving.

Exercise 7.3 *Force-field analysis*

Purpose
To give a framework for making an action plan

Procedure
The group splits into pairs. One person identifies a problem that they have that they have not resolved. Remind the group that it is not advisable to work with a very sensitive issue. For example, Sally, a member of the group, identifies her problem as: 'I don't feel very confident.' Her partner, Jane, helps her to work on the problem using force-field analysis. The first step is to formulate a clear goal. What is it that Sally would like to achieve. She says: 'I want to go to a party and enjoy it.'
Jane then draws the force-field analysis (Figure 7.1) and helps Sally to identify facilitating and hindering forces that prevent her from achieving her goal. The lines are shorter or longer depending on the strength of the force. Generating upwards from the problem, they note the helping forces, for example, 'I have a lovely dress I want to wear to parties.' A very long arrow would indicate that the force was great; a shorter one would indicate that the force was small in affecting the situation. Once the diagram has been drawn, this can form the basis for discussion of ways to decrease the hindering forces and enhance the facilitating forces. The pair note what action plan might be formulated and negotiate a way to keep accounts of progress.

Debriefing
In the pair, discuss the process of analysing the forces that enable you to act and those that prevent action. Do not forget to explore the forces that cannot be changed or that present particular difficulty.

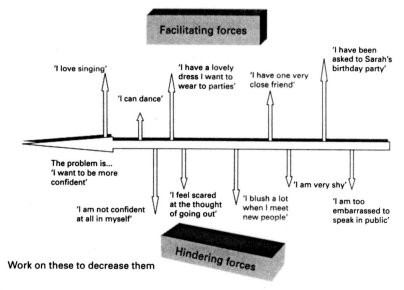

Figure 7.1 *Force-field analysis in action*

Exercise 7.4 *Selecting an alternative and making a plan*

Purpose
To learn to listen carefully to another person as they formulate a plan of action that feels right for them.
To practise the skills of facilitating choices.

Procedure
The group forms into threes. You have prepared vignettes that build on the explorations of alternatives in the previous exercise. For example:

> Speaker: 'My family is moving away to another town. I am really scared and will miss my friends so much. Mum and Dad do not seem to have noticed.'

After questioning, the speaker has explored a number of possibilities, including the following options:

- telling Mum and Dad that he is very upset about the move;
- telling his best friends that he would like to see them after the move;
- planning ways of keeping in touch by meeting in the holidays;
- finding out about his new school.

The supporter and the speaker select one of these options. The supporter asks questions like:

> 'When will you do this?'
> 'When will you tell me how it went?'

The observer notes how the interaction is going and gives feedback about aspects that were helpful and aspects that were not.

Debriefing

This exercise gives an opportunity to explore the process of facilitating change in the client. It is helpful to talk about the difficulties that may be encountered in taking action and the need to be supportive if it does not always succeed. It is also an opportunity to explore the importance of not being judgemental about the client's proposed action plans.

Exercise 7.5 *Evaluating the results of the action*

Purpose

To evaluate how the action plan went.

Procedure

Peer supporters bring their own issues to the group where they have actually attempted, through an action plan, to make changes in order to overcome a real problem. (As mentioned earlier in the chapter, these problems should not be too sensitive. **Remember that the participants meet and work with one another every day.**) In small groups, those who are able/willing to share this experience respond to questions from other members of the group.
Examples of questions that can be used include:

'How did it go?'
'What happened?'
'Are there any ways in which you wish that you could have done it differently?'
'Shall we discuss these options now?'
'How are you dealing with the changes?'

Debriefing

This exercise gives an opportunity to explore the outcomes of action and the changes that ensue, some of which will be unexpected. It is helpful to talk about the difficulties that may be encountered in taking action and the need to be supportive if it does not always succeed. It is also an opportunity to explore the importance of not being judgemental about the client's proposed action plans.

Exercise 7.6 *Describing and owning feelings*

Purpose

To encourage each person in the group to identify and own their individual feelings.

Procedure

Divide the large group into pairs. The pairs decide which one is to be A, the describer, and which one is to be B, the listener. A is given a set of unfinished sentences to complete, each describing how a person feels in a range of contexts, for example:

A: 'When people are nice to me, I feel . . . '.

After each sentence, B paraphrases what A said. Suggested sentences are:

'When no-one speaks to me, I feel. . . . '; 'When people are nasty to me, I feel . . . '; 'When people put me down, I feel. . . . '; 'When I am unappreciated, I feel. . . . '; 'When I am excluded from a group, I feel. . . . '; 'When I am the odd one out, I feel. . . . ' 'When someone praises me, I feel. . . . '

Halfway through, the roles are reversed, and the same unfinished sentences are completed by B with A as listener.

Debriefing

In the large group, ask people to comment not on the content of their partner's statements, but on the feelings. Discuss which feelings were easier to describe than others, and explore what the implications are for their work as peer supporters. An example may be that it is hard to talk about being excluded from a group because there is some shame in sharing the experience of rejection. Discuss the range of words that can be used to paraphrase a feeling.

This is an opportunity to explore whether there are some emotions that members of the group find it hard to talk about. Do not forget to include some discussion about silence. When a person cannot find words to describe their pain, it can be helpful for the peer supporter to acknowledge this by using phrases like:

'It must be hard to find words to express what you are feeling.'

This is also an opportunity for peer supporters to experience directly the importance of a vocabulary of the emotions for their work.

Exercise 7.7 *Communicating that you understand the other's point of view* (based on an exercise designed by Egan, 1990, p. 40)

Purpose

To give peer supporters the opportunity to practise the skill of listening with empathy to what a person says and to communicate that empathy.

Procedure

The group divides into threes in which the roles are listener, speaker and observer. Each speaker is given a short time to prepare a statement on an

issue of importance to him or her. The statements must be short enough to
be made within one minute. The group decides which person is to speak
first. The speaker then delivers the statement to the listener. The observer
watches in silence. The listener waits until the speaker has finished and then
summarizes what has been said. The listener must begin with the phrase
'These are your words as I heard them.'

The speaker may state: 'There are these boys and they keep commenting on
the fact that I am shy. I can't help it that I am shy and I have tried and tried
to be more outgoing, but nobody seems to appreciate this and they just
laugh at me all the time. I feel so upset and now dread coming into a room
for fear of what other people are going to say.'

The listener summarizes as follows: 'These are your words as I heard them.
You are really angry at these boys because they do not see you as a person.
They do not understand you as you are. You now find it hard to go into
places where other people are because you think that they will also not see
you as you are, and that is very upsetting.'

Debriefing

Within the threesome, the observer asks the speaker questions like, 'Did it
feel right to say that you were angry at these boys?' and 'Did it help to hear
that other people did not see you as you are?' The speaker is encouraged to
comment on whether the summary was helpful and to discuss ways in which
it might have been different. Since each person has the opportunity to
experience the three roles, the exercise provides scope for giving and
receiving constructive feedback on sensitive responsiveness and the
expression of empathy.

Exercise 7.8 *Statues of anger (adapted from Fine and Macbeth, 1992a, p. 95)*

Purpose

To make links between anger and hate.
To turn understanding of an emotion into a visual expression.

Procedure

The facilitator prepares a set of index cards. On half of them write 'anger'
on one side, 'hate' and 'aggression' on the other side. On the remaining
cards write 'hurt' on one side, 'bitterness' and 'resentment' on the other.
Divide the group into pairs. Each pair is given one card, so that half of the
group will be working on anger and the other half on hurt. In each pair one
person (A) moulds their partner (B) into a statue which expresses the key
word. Next, B moulds A into a statue which expresses the words on the
other side of the same card. Pick some of these statues to comment on.
Look at them as pairs, and encourage observation from the rest of the
group. Which statue is expressing which emotion? Ask each statue how they
are feeling in their chosen position.

Debriefing

Discuss the connections between hurt and bitterness, and between anger and hate. Are there ways in which anger might be used positively? What happens to pain that we try to push away? Does it remain in the form of bitterness or resentment? What happens to anger that is not acknowledged? Does it turn into aggression and hate?

Exercise 7.9 *Facing anger (adapted from Fine and Macbeth, 1992a, p. 98)*

Purpose

To practise receiving someone's anger and helping them to transform it into constructive action.

To practise planning a strategy before taking action.

To practise observing a partner's performance and the giving of constructive feedback.

Procedure

The facilitator gives participants role cards in which a person unleashed their anger on another person, for example in the supermarket, in a queue, in class. In the whole group, individuals take it in turns to be either the angry person or the person who is the object of the anger. Observers report back on what they see. What was said? How did the angry person approach the other? How did the other person respond? Was the response appropriate? Members of the group then ask each of the actors how they feel and what their motives were. Questions can include: What did you feel at that moment? Why do you think that he/she did that? Why did you respond in that way? Was there any hurt behind that anger?

Participants are then asked to enact their role plays to demonstrate alternative ways of responding; in particular, ways that influence the interchange constructively. The audience observe closely and, again, ask questions about feelings and motives.

In the whole group, all the participants look at the techniques and responses that emerged from the role-plays, and discuss their appropriateness.

Debriefing

How did participants feel about their in-role performance? What did they learn by taking part and observing? How did the feedback from observers help the participants to understand what had occurred?

Exercise 7.10 *Responding to conflict (adapted from Cole, 1987, p. 45)*

Purpose

To increase participants' awareness of the four basic responses to conflict.

To familiarize participants with some specific skills for successfully resolving conflict situations.

Procedure

The facilitator makes a brief presentation on the nature of conflict. Then, on flip-chart paper, brainstorms with the group the possible conflicts that occur in their context, e.g. peer versus peer; adult versus young person; manager versus employee. Selecting some examples from their own experience, the group discuss the four basic responses to conflict – fight, avoidance, compromise and problem-solving – with reference to the conflict situations that they have chosen. The outcomes of each response are explored, as are the feelings that arise for each party in the conflict.

Debriefing

By engaging in this discussion with the group, the facilitator creates an opportunity to begin to explore the skills of conflict resolution. Themes to explore at this stage include: how to build trust; how to identify the problem; how to introduce the idea of exploring alternatives; and how to make a plan.

Exercise 7.11 *Changing the outcome (adapted from Fine and Macbeth, 1992a, p. 89)*

Purpose

To change participants' experience of being powerless in a given situation. To try out alternative lines of action and evaluate their effect.

Procedure

Participants are asked to think of a situation in which someone might feel powerless. (It is best if the situation does not concern something that is too personal for participants.) It could be a situation in which that person wished that they had been able to act differently.

In groups of three, each person sculpts the rest of the group into three tableaux that depict the beginning, the middle and the end of the situation. This is carried out in silence. When all the members of the threesome have completed their tableau, they decide on **one** that they will do more work on. The tableaux are run again for the chosen story, but this time each of the characters has one spoken thought in each tableau. The thoughts should be spoken in a pre-determined order, as decided by the threesome. Members of the whole group are asked to suggest ways in which the powerless person could have acted differently. Members of the whole group try out these suggestions with the person who has the new idea entering into the tableau and playing the person whose actions they want to change.

Debriefing

By discussing the effect of different actions on an outcome, the facilitator creates an opportunity for the whole group to explore the idea of changing the scripts of an episode in someone's life. The group are encouraged to consider what they personally will take away with them from this exercise.

Exercise 7.12 *Smouldering in the peer group (adapted from Fine and Macbeth, 1992a, p. 86)*

Purpose
To increase participants' awareness of tensions and potential difficulties in peer relationships.

To familiarize participants with some specific skills for successfully resolving conflict within the peer group.

Procedure
In small groups, participants in turn create a tableau of what happens in young people's relationships. In the larger group, each smaller group presents its tableau.

Members of the large group say what tensions and difficulties they observe. Each figure in the tableau is asked what they are feeling in a word – e.g. 'sad', 'angry', 'rejected'.

Debriefing
In the large group, members discuss such questions as: Where are the potential points of conflict? What, if anything, is smouldering in each picture? Finally, the groups discuss ways in which potentially difficult situations might be moved forward to possible solutions.

Exercise 7.13 *What do we do? (adapted from Fine and Macbeth, 1992a, p. 33)*

Purpose
To increase participants' insights into the range of responses that exist within the group.

To make connections among the responses.

Procedure
The facilitator invites the group to consider their usual responses to situations of conflict. What feelings do they experience when there is a conflict? Participants are asked to write their responses down on a piece of paper. After 10 minutes (or when everyone has finished), participants are asked to read their list aloud one by one. Then comments are invited.

Debriefing
This is an opportunity to share common patterns in the ways in which the group responds to conflict, for example patterns of gender or of ethnicity. Explore what are the most frequent themes and those that are least common. Do people in the group think of conflict as something interpersonal, intra-group or inter-group? Does anyone in the group respond positively or with enjoyment to conflict? Why? Is there any potential within the group to look at conflict as a positive force for change?

PART IV

MONITORING AND EVALUATING THE SYSTEM

8

ETHICS AND THE LAW

One of the concerns most often expressed by those who question the value of peer support is that young people may 'make matters worse'. Our experience does not suggest that this is a common occurrence. Nevertheless, it is a valid concern that we ignore at our peril. The bottom line is that you as the adult involved in managing/supervising young people who are peer supporters are responsible for any action they take or do not take. It is important, therefore, that you be familiar with relevant ethical and legal issues and understand their implications for your peer support service. In addition, you will need to develop guidelines to aid peer supporters in knowing what and when to refer to you, and you will need to ensure that your peer supporters can apply these guidelines in practice. This chapter will outline the areas of law and ethics with which you need to be familiar, and some ways of helping young people understand their implications in practice.

The law

Law and its interpretation is a complex and constantly changing subject. For this reason, our intention in this section is simply to alert you to the areas of law with which you, or at least your organization, should be familiar if you are setting up a peer support service. For further detail and interpretation of the law as it applies to counselling (which is similar to peer support in its requirements), we would recommend consulting either Jenkins (1997) or Bond (1993). The sections on law in this chapter are based in part on the writings of Jenkins, but the interpretations are the authors' own.

There are three main areas of law in the UK which influence services provided to and by young people. They are:

- **statute law:** (that is, law by legislation), which includes the Mental Health Act (1983), the Suicide Act (1961) and the Children Act (1989);
- **common law:** (that is, law based primarily on established principles and practice), which includes law on confidentiality;
- **case law:** (that is, law based on a specific case in which a particular principle of law is clarified), which includes the well-known case of *Gillick* v. *West Norfolk Area Health Authority* (1986), which concerned the rights of mature but minor children to give consent to medical treatment.

The following Acts of Parliament are those most likely to influence your decisions about policies and practices within a peer support service:

- **Suicide Act (1961):** This permits charges under criminal law for 'aiding and abetting a suicide' of any person who actively assists a suicide or who is aware of the intention to commit suicide and does not inform an appropriate professional as defined under the Mental Health Act.
- **Mental Health Act (1983)** (but undergoing revisions at time of going to press): This permits compulsory admission to hospital by two designated professionals (approved social worker, psychiatrist, the person's general practitioner) in clearly defined circumstances, which must include the person being a danger to him/herself or others.
- **Children Act (1989):** This imposes a duty on workers in local authorities, education authorities, housing authorities, health authorities and others authorized by the Secretary of State to provide relevant information to assist inquiries into child welfare, except 'where doing so would be unreasonable in all the circumstances of the case'.

Implications of the law for peer support services

Very simply, the implications for peer support services are as follows: young people using a peer support service should be offered confidentiality except in the circumstances specified in the three Acts of Parliament listed above. These circumstances are detailed in our section on confidentiality. The Gillick principle (1986) allows for young people under the age of 16 years to consent to medical procedures (these have been loosely defined to include counselling, for example) if a mature level of understanding can be proven. Some youth counselling and sexual health services make use of this ruling to allow young people to use their services without parental consent. However, schools, in our experience, generally have a policy of involving parents for issues to do with any under-age young person and sometimes any young person who attends the school, regardless of age. Our sections on boundaries and confidentiality incorporate the requirements of the law. However, as some issues may vary depending upon your setting (such as the need or not for parental consent as described above), it is important that you familiarize yourself with the policies and practices of your school or other organization before setting procedures for your peer support service. (See also Daniels and Jenkins, 2000.)

Ethics

Ethical guidelines developed for counsellors and those using counselling skills are useful in considering the ethical issues likely to arise in a peer support service. The British Association for Counselling provides a general code of ethics (BAC, 1997) and specific guidelines on confidentiality (BAC, 1994) which may be helpful to refer to.

Boundaries

One of the main ethical issues which it is important to address in relation to the peer support service is that of boundaries. We find it helpful to look at it in terms of different types of boundaries: role boundaries; relationship boundaries; and boundaries regarding types of problems.

Role boundaries

It is important that roles and responsibilities of peer supporters be clearly defined and understood by peer supporters themselves, service-users and any adults who may refer young people to the service. Without clarity, peer supporters may feel pressure to take on something they are not experienced or mature enough to handle, possibly with serious consequences. See Example 8.1 for an illustration.

Example 8.1

A teacher sends a young person who is seriously depressed and actually in need of professional help to the peer support service because she doesn't have time to arrange a professional referral herself. The peer supporter who sees this depressed young person feels pressurized by the young person's desperation and by the teacher's apparent belief that a peer supporter should be able to cope with the problem. Rather than admit that the problem is too severe for peer support, he tries to help the young person but the young person only becomes more distressed and despairing.

The role of peer supporter should be a limited but valuable one – that is, caring about, listening, helping people find their own solutions. Peer supporters and the adults around them need to understand the dangers of exceeding these limits.

Relationship boundaries

It is important that peer supporters be helped to differentiate between a helping relationship and a friendship. This is particularly true for peer support services that are based on a counselling model, but is relevant in varying degrees for all models of peer support. At the very least, peer supporters need to understand that when they are in their peer support role, the other person's needs are the focus of the interaction. This is, of course, different from a social interaction in which either person's needs may be paramount at any one time. This differentiation is particularly complex to negotiate in an environment such as a school or a youth club where peer supporters may be supporting someone with whom they have close and frequent contact on a different basis (for example, someone who shares classes with them). The following are some ways in which peer supporters can be helped to maintain appropriate boundaries.

- Having the practice of establishing and maintaining boundaries of time and place to indicate the helping nature of the peer support relationship to the person seeking help. See Example 8.2.

Example 8.2

Some services have a peer support room and specific times when peer supporters are available there. Other services have badges for their peer supporters to wear when 'on duty'. Services which employ 'creative loitering' sometimes suggest that peer supporters introduce themselves as such at the beginning of a helping interaction.

- Encouraging peer supporters to recognize their own needs, normalizing them and providing a structure (for example, supervision or debriefing) through which their needs can be addressed. See Example 8.3.

Example 8.3

Anna, a peer supporter whose brother died in a car accident the previous year, was approached by Louise, whose mother was seriously ill and about whom she was constantly anxious. Anna was able to speak in supervision about how upsetting she found supporting Louise but how guilty she would feel if she let her down as she, herself, had had no-one to talk to when her brother was killed. Anna was helped by talking about her own feelings and by the group agreeing that another peer supporter would also make herself available to help Louise so that the burden did not fall only on Anna, for whom it raised many personal issues about the death of a loved one.

- Teaching peer supporters to recognize signs that indicate they are becoming too involved or the person seeking help is becoming too dependent on them, and ensuring they know what to do about it. See Example 8.4.

Example 8.4

A peer supporter is supporting a girl who is being bullied by some older girls. One day when she is particularly upset, he finds himself giving her his home telephone number to ring 'in case she needs it'. He knows that peer supporters are not supposed to offer to help people outside of school time and he knows that he needs to talk about the fact that he did so in supervision. When he does, he is helped to think about his reasons for breaking this rule and to plan a way of addressing it with the girl whom he is helping.

Boundaries regarding types of problems
Whilst peer supporters may intervene helpfully on a wide range of issues, there are some problems which should never be handled by peer supporters alone. Problems which should have the involvement of the adult supervisor/manager are those in which there is a serious possibility of harm to the person seeking help or another person. The most common examples of this are: sexual or physical abuse; suicide threats or attempts; serious self-harm; and mental illness.

Peer supporters should know that in the circumstances described above, they must always seek help immediately from the adult(s) responsible for the service. In addition, they should be encouraged to seek help whenever they feel beyond their depth. They will need to be taught to differentiate between situations that require immediate adult guidance and those which can wait until the next scheduled supervision or debriefing session. See Example 8.5.

Example 8.5

Emma, a peer supporter, has been spending some time with a younger girl who always seems uncared for and unhappy. In the course of one of their conversations, the younger girl says she is upset because her step-father often locks her in the cupboard as punishment for not doing the housework. Emma knows that this is potentially a serious situation and she follows the agreed school procedure of telling the younger girl that she would like to mention this to the teacher who manages the peer support service. She then goes to the staff room and asks to speak urgently with the teacher responsible. The potential abuse/neglect issue is then taken on by the teacher while Emma is able to continue her role as a peer supporter of the young girl.

Confidentiality

The other ethical issue of significance in peer support is confidentiality. Even for trained professionals, this can be a difficult issue to understand and negotiate in all its permutations; therefore it is important to spend some time ensuring that peer supporters understand exactly what is required in a range of circumstances.

When training peer supporters, we usually start by asking them about their understanding of confidentiality. One way of approaching this is to brainstorm what the issue means and to write all the aspects of confidentiality mentioned on a sheet of paper. This is then used as a basis for a definition of what confidentiality means in the circumstances in which your peer supporters will be working. In our experience, young people are quite perceptive about the complexities of confidentiality, as illustrated by the young man who described it as 'not telling something personal you know about someone even when you've had a fight with him and you feel he has treated you unfairly'. Try to create a definition that describes exactly what is expected of your peer supporters and of you as the adult responsible. See Box 8.1 for an example of a working definition of confidentiality.

There need to be clear guidelines on when confidentiality must be broken. Many services have these written down and available to be consulted by peer supporters whenever they need guidance in this area. See Box 8.2 for an example of such guidelines.

Finally, peer supporters will need to have a process for conveying the confidentiality agreement to people who come to them for help. Some services have the agreement posted, others have it written on a sheet of paper which is handed to the person seeking help, and still others encourage peer supporters to discuss it with the person before talking about their problem. One advantage of the 'posting' or 'hand-out' methods is that time

Box 8.1 *A working definition of confidentiality for a peer support service*

- Everything said to you in your role as a peer supporter should be kept to yourself.

- In supervision/debriefing, speak about the issues raised but do not disclose information that would identify the individual.

- If records are kept, write them immediately and put them in the locked place where they are stored. Do not take them away with you.

- Only identify the individual who has sought your help in the circumstances agreed in your peer support service and then only to the adult(s) responsible for the peer support service.

Box 8.2 *Guidelines for breaking confidentiality*

You will need to break confidentiality if, at any time, the health or safety of the person seeking your help or any other person is at risk.

1. Situations in which confidentiality will need to be broken:
- There is disclosure or evidence of physical, sexual or serious emotional abuse or neglect.
- Suicide is threatened or attempted.
- There is disclosure or evidence of serious self-harm (including drug or alcohol misuse that may be life-threatening).
- There is evidence of serious mental illness.

2. What to do if confidentiality needs to be broken:
- Discuss with the person seeking your help the need to break confidentiality and encourage him/her to speak to a responsible adult him/herself.
- Discuss the situation with the adult(s) responsible for the peer support service, preferably with the person's consent but even if s/he does not consent (with or without the person present).
- The adult(s) responsible for the peer support service will decide what action is needed and who needs to be informed, and they will keep a written record of all action taken.
- You and/or the adult responsible should discuss with the person seeking help any action taken and then continue to support him/her.

does not need to be taken up explaining something which may be of little interest to the person who has come for help with their problem. However, telling them in person ensures that they have heard and understood the confidentiality of the service and its limitations. It can be a difficult task to explain all the limitations of confidentiality in a way that does not discourage the young person from disclosing anything at all about themselves! If you choose to use this method, then we would recommend having peer supporters practise a simple statement such as:

> Everything you say here will be just between us. The only time I would have to tell anyone else is if you or someone else were in danger and then I would only tell Ms X [the adult responsible for the peer support service]. We meet as a group sometimes, but we don't talk about individual people, just some of the problems they bring to us.

Young people will not use a peer support service if they are unsure about levels of confidentiality. Therefore, the need for peer supporters to follow these guidelines cannot be emphasized enough. One way of helping peer supporters keep confidentiality is to give them some scenarios based on real-life situations on which to practise. Exercise 8.1 provides some suitable scenarios and describes a group process for examining them.

Clarity about legal and ethical issues relevant to peer support is important in the planning and day-to-day management of a peer support service. Chapter 9 will demonstrate how it is also needed in the supervision of peer supporters.

Exercise 8.1 *Keeping confidentiality: what do I do if . . . ?*

Purpose
To provide an opportunity to practise situations in which it may be difficult to keep confidentiality.

Procedure
Divide young people into small groups (three or four) and ask them to consider the following situations.
Ask them to come up with responses that would not break confidentiality.
Ask them to think about whether there is any other action they should take.

Debriefing
In the whole group, discuss the scenarios one by one and have each group present their response to a particular scenario.
Compare the responses and look at the advantages and disadvantages of each.
Be prepared to offer a suitable response if needed, once the groups have offered theirs.

Scenarios for Exercise 8.1

Scenario 1

Someone who you know is a good friend of the person who came to you for help says to you: 'I'm really concerned about Julie. I know she is unhappy and she told me she went to talk to you about it. If you tell me what the problem is, perhaps I can help her. You know I'm her best friend.'

Sample response: 'I know you just want to help, but you know I'm not allowed to say anything about people I see as a peer supporter.'

If you see Julie again as a peer supporter, you might also want to tell her that her friend was asking you about her and sound out whether she feels that friend could be a support to her in her current situation.

Scenario 2

Julie's teacher stops you in the corridor and says: 'I noticed in the peer support appointment book that Julie came to talk to you yesterday. I've noticed that she seems upset these days. Perhaps you could give me some idea what the problem is so that I could try to help.'

Sample response: 'I'm sorry but I'm not allowed to say anything about what people tell me as a peer supporter. Maybe you should talk to Ms X, who is in charge of the service, and she could give you some advice.'

NB: In this case, you would also want to talk to Ms X yourself, as teachers not involved with the peer support service should not have access to the peer support appointments book!

Scenario 3

You meet Julie's mum in the shops and she says to you: 'Aren't you in Julie's class? Have you any idea why she seems so unhappy with school these days? She doesn't seem to want to talk to me about it, but I thought maybe one of her friends could tell me.'

Sample response: 'I don't really know Mrs J. Maybe she just needs a bit of time before she can talk to you if something is bothering her.'

If you see Julie again as a peer supporter, you should tell her that her mother had stopped you and asked if you knew what the problem was. You could assure Julie that you had not told her mother but take the opportunity to explore with her whether or not she could tell her mother and maybe get her help with the problem.

Scenario 4

Julie has been telling you about how she is being bullied by a gang of girls. She thinks she saw one of them with a knife. You know these girls and the one she thought had a knife is someone you know quite well. You are worried about what to do; whether to tell the adult who supervises the peer supporters or not. When you get home, your mother says: ' You seem worried. What's wrong? Do you want to tell me about it?'

Sample response: Yes, I am worried about something I was told about some bullying at school. But it was told to me in confidence so I can't tell you the details. I'll go and see Ms X tomorrow and she'll be able to sort it out.'

You do need to talk to Ms X if you feel you are out of your depth. One way of knowing you are out of your depth is when you find yourself really wanting to tell someone about what was said to you in confidence.

Scenario 5

One of your good friends is also a peer supporter and you know that he fancies Julie. He knows that she has come to see you and he is interested to know what happened. He says: 'I see you saw Julie today. What did she talk about? It's all right to tell me since we're both peer supporters.'

Sample response: 'You know I can't tell you what she said. We're only allowed to talk about that kind of thing in supervision. Anyway, it's even worse because you fancy her, so it wouldn't be fair to her.'

You might want to raise the general issue in supervision to clarify whether or not you should talk to other peer supporters about people who come to see you outside of supervision. The answer should be 'no' unless your peer support service has a buddying structure in which you talk it over only with your agreed buddy before bringing it to your supervisor.

9

SUPERVISION

We have chosen to use the counselling term 'supervision' to describe the act of reflecting on one's work with the help of peers and/or someone with more experience and training in the work. Some people in the peer support field prefer to use the term 'debriefing' as this has a less formal, less counselling jargon sound to it. For the purposes of peer support, the activities of supervising or debriefing are sufficiently similar to be interchangeable. Therefore, in this chapter, for the sake of simplicity, we will use the term 'supervision' to encompass both.

The importance of supervision

We cannot overemphasize the importance of regular supervision or debriefing for peer supporters. In our work with a wide range of peer support services we have found this to be one of the most significant factors in creating a safe, effective support service and in keeping a service going during the periods when peer supporters might otherwise lose motivation and commitment. In their report to the Prince's Trust on the effectiveness of peer support systems in challenging school bullying, based on questionnaire and interview information from 54 secondary schools and colleges, Naylor and Cowie (1998, p. 26) recommend that:

> all schools need to ensure that the peer supporters are provided with frequent and regular opportunities for being debriefed about their supporting experiences. In other words, there needs to be recognition that the peer supporters themselves need continual support from the teachers if they are to be successful in their own supporting roles.

We are aware that many of the adults managing and supervising these services are doing this in their own time in addition to their regular jobs. And we know that this makes it very difficult for them to find regular time to meet with their peer supporters for supervision. However, it is a case, in our view, of spending time to save time. Dealing with a mishandled boundary or confidentiality issue will take much more time in the end than offering regular supervision, and has the added disadvantage of bringing the entire service into disrepute. Given that the provision of supervision is such an important indicator of success and safety, it is important for the adults involved to be honest with themselves from the beginning. If there is really not enough time to supervise peer supporters regularly, perhaps it is not the best time to set up a peer support service.

In order to plan and run supervision sessions in the most effective and efficient manner possible, it is necessary to consider several factors: the functions of supervision; models of supervision available; the qualities needed to make a good supervisor; and some ways of structuring super-vision sessions. These will be discussed in the following sections of this chapter. For those who wish to read further on supervision, Carroll (1996) and Hawkins and Shohet (1989) may be helpful.

The functions of supervision

We are aware that the word 'supervision' is often linked in people's minds to the idea of having someone senior in the hierarchy watching and criticizing their work, but this is not at all the meaning we want peer supporters or their supervisors to associate with it. Instead, we want peer support service managers, supervisors and peer supporters to associate supervision with its more positive learning, guiding and supportive functions. The primary function of supervision must always be to ensure the welfare of service-users. Whatever other needs supervision may meet, it is absolutely essential that, as its first and foremost function, it protects the best interests of the young people using the peer support service. In the case of peer support, supervision is also designed to develop the skills of the peer supporters and to provide emotional support to them. Super-vision can also have a great deal of 'added value' in that it can be a forum for monitoring the effectiveness of the service, a forum in which ideas for further training sessions can be generated, and, if done in a group, it can help develop cohesiveness within the group of peer supporters. It is useful to bear all of these functions in mind when planning supervision/debriefing sessions.

Models of supervision

Within the counselling field there are a number of possible models of supervision to choose from, including: supervision using audio- or video-tapes of sessions; live supervision using the supervisor in the room or behind a two-way mirror; and reported supervision. Peer support services almost universally choose the last of these as it is the simplest and least intrusive model and requires no special equipment. Whilst this is a perfectly reasonable and practical decision, it is important to bear in mind that reported supervision has a significant weakness – it relies entirely on the accuracy of recall and willingness to disclose of the peer supporter reporting on his/her session. Therefore, it is important for anyone supervising to remember that reported supervision can never be 'the truth'; it is always only one individual's account of 'the truth' as he or she experiences it. Nevertheless, a peer supporter's report of what has happened in a supporting session can provide much useful information.

Within the reported supervision model, there are two options for peer support services:

- group supervision facilitated by an adult supervisor;
- individual supervision with an adult supervisor.

The third possibility, peer group supervision, used by some professional counsellors, is not an option due to the lack of maturity and legal accountability of young peer supporters. The majority of services we have known offer group supervision, but some provide individual supervision and a few employ both models. To assist managers and supervisors in choosing the best model for their service, here is a summary of the advantages of each, based on our experience.

The advantages of group supervision are:

- It models the use of peer support in that group members are encouraged to help one another find answers to the problems raised.
- It is an effective use of the supervisor's time as he or she can supervise several peer supporters at once.
- It facilitates learning from the strengths and weaknesses of others.
- It develops cohesiveness within the group which can sustain the peer supporters through difficult times such as poor uptake or lack of support from staff.
- It provides the opportunity for group exercises such as a role-play of a situation which a particular peer supporter has found difficult.

The advantages of individual supervision are:

- It can be adjusted to suit the particular needs of the individual peer supporter.
- It offers an experience of one-to-one support, thus modelling an interaction similar to the one the peer supporter is offering to the young people who come to him or her for help.
- It may result in peer supporters feeling more attended to and thus result in more confident, supported peer supporters.
- It provides greater confidentiality for the peer supporter and therefore may result in more honesty about difficulties the peer supporter is experiencing in his or her support work. (However, it is also possible that an individual meeting with an adult would feel threatening and therefore less conducive to self-disclosure.)

It will probably be clear from the lists above that neither model is necessarily better than the other. If well done, either provides adequate protection for service-users, and good learning and support for peer supporters. Whichever model is used, it will also be necessary to have arrangements for peer supporters to contact one of the adults responsible for the service outside of the regular supervision arrangements should an urgent issue arise. Most supervisors choose a model that suits the amount of time they have available, the number of peer supporters they need to supervise, and the skills they feel they have.

The qualities of a good supervisor

Many teachers, youth workers, social workers, school counsellors and others who decide to set up a peer support service will not have provided supervision before. Fortunately, supervision at this fairly basic level usually requires skills already used by these professionals in other aspects of their work. As might be expected, the qualities of a good peer support supervisor are not so very different from the qualities of a good peer supporter! For the most part a supervisor will need the skills of listening, facilitating disclosure, focusing and providing boundaries and guidance in a non-judgemental way. In addition, it will be important to model some of the behaviours desirable in a peer supporter such as willingness to admit to not knowing or to making a mistake, appropriate emotional openness, and caring without over-involvement. For those who feel comfortable handling groups of young people, this may be the model of choice. For those who feel more confident in one-to-one relationships, the individual supervision model may be more suitable. Whatever your strengths or weaknesses, remember that supervision, like peer support, does not need to be perfect. It only needs to be good enough.

Structuring supervision sessions

When we are training people to set up, manage and supervise peer support services, we normally begin the session on supervision by asking them to do two exercises. As they are designed to help people think concretely about how they would structure their supervision sessions, they might be useful to try on your own or with the other adults who will be jointly responsible for your peer support service. So before reading on, try Exercises 9.1 and 9.2.

Probably the only practical way of structuring individual supervision for 16 peer supporters in two hours a week is to see each person for half an hour once a month. However, this really is a minimal amount of contact. If your peer supporters are supporting people regularly, it is unlikely to provide adequate support for them, and if they are not seeing people or you regularly, there is a risk of them losing interest in the service altogether. Therefore, the short answer is that it would almost certainly be better to offer group supervision more often than individual supervision too infrequently. If you have only eight peer supporters, then individual supervision is more practical. Seeing each person for half an hour every two weeks is probably enough to deal with most supervision issues. However, it is worth mentioning that you will also need to have 'business' meetings with the whole group in addition. Half an hour is not long for someone to tell you about the support they have been offering and the problems they have encountered. It is important to keep the session focused. By the end of a supervision session, you should have answers to the following questions:

- How are they feeling about their peer support work, with this person and in general?
- Do they have any particular concerns about any aspect of their peer support work that you should know about? (You might remind them of the type of ethical issue they need to tell you about.)
- Who have they been supporting? (This does not require identification of the individual – 'a girl in Year 10' would do.)
- How much time have they spent doing it?
- What is the problem this person has brought to the peer supporter?
- What has the peer supporter done with it so far?
- What has been the outcome of their intervention to date?
- What do they intend to do next, if anything?

Having answers to these questions does not mean that you need to ask the questions directly. Often a more open: 'So what's been happening with your peer support in the last two weeks?' and a few prompts will produce more information than will direct questioning.

If you have 12 or more peer supporters and two hours or less a week, then group supervision is probably the best model. It is possible to supervise a group of 12, but not much more than that. It is probably best to make two smaller groups and for each to meet weekly. It is important to structure sessions so that anyone with a serious concern has a chance to raise it and have help with it. It is also important that the time is not regularly taken by the same one or two individuals. Clear structures, firm time-keeping and skillful group facilitation will be needed to make the most of these sessions. The following is a format we have used with large groups. It has the advantage of teaching through example, a problem-solving style that is likely to be helpful to the young people in their peer support work.

A format for group supervision

Begin with a 'go-round' in which everyone tells the group about the peer support they have done since the last meeting. Ensure that everyone speaks, even if only to say that they have not done any peer support since last time. In group supervision, it is important that every member feels a part of the group, and one way to achieve this is to ensure that everyone contributes at least once. The 'go-round' is the time when anyone should say if they want help with a situation they are finding difficult. Each person should speak for only two or three minutes. In introducing the 'go-round' it is important to explain that this is not the time to describe a problem, but the time to simply let the group know if they have one.

Spend a minimum of half the session on difficulties that peer supporters have raised. This can take the form of the peer supporter describing the situation (remind him/her about not giving any identifying information or extraneous detail) and the supervisor asking the group to help him/her think about it. The supervisor could ask, for example:

> Does anyone have any ideas about what the person seeking help might be feeling?

> Can anyone guess why what the peer supporter did didn't work?

After some discussion, offer a clear summing up such as:

> Let's look at where we've got to now. Peer Supporter, what are you going to do next time you meet this person?

Or

> Peer Supporter, what have you learned from this situation that you can use another time?

In group supervision, another way of addressing difficulties a peer supporter is having is to ask a peer supporter to 'be' the person he or she is supporting. Then ask another peer supporter, or perhaps two in succession, to try to work with him/her on the problem. This allows the peer supporter to see other ways of working with the issue and the person. The acting out of the problem often demonstrates something about the cause or nature of the problem or about why an intervention is not helping which is not evident in a purely verbal account. This format also gives other peer supporters the chance to be actively involved in the group, even if they have nothing specific to bring.

Attendance

A question which is often raised during our trainings is whether or not peer supporters should be required to attend supervision sessions. There is no absolute answer to this, but several factors mitigate in favour of a minimum attendance requirement. First, in general, it is the young people who attend supervision regularly who remain committed to the peer support service. Second, the group needs consistent membership and regular participation in order to function well. Third, if the supervision group is running well, then the more often peer supporters attend and find that they learn something, the more they will want to attend. And finally, you are accountable for the support your peer supporters are offering whether or not they attend supervision and whether or not you know what they are doing. For all of these reasons, an attendance requirement is probably a good idea. Having said that, it is entirely possible to run a supervision group that peer supporters are so keen to attend that you never need to enforce the attendance requirement.

Desired outcomes of supervision

At the end of any supervision session, whether group or individual, you want your peer supporters to go away feeling contained, heard, supported and guided. (Note that this is the same way you want people using the peer support service to feel after a meeting with their peer supporter.) They should feel positive about the work they have done and helped to go on doing it. They should also feel challenged to think about how they could improve their support for another time. There is never a time when a peer supporter should leave supervision feeling criticized or unsupported. Even if someone has done something that clearly is unhelpful, it will be more useful to them and to the other peer supporters if you can make it a learning experience. Making a learning experience out of an apparent disaster can tax the imagination, but it does demonstrate that solutions are possible even in the most unlikely of circumstances! This does not, of course, preclude taking firm action to stop a young person from continuing as a peer supporter if you feel this is warranted.

Practising supervision knowledge and skills

There are three separate but inter-related areas of supervision knowledge and skills that a potential supervisor will need to develop. The first of these involves recognizing and dealing with ethical dilemmas. Exercise 9.3 provides the opportunity for supervisors to consider, in advance, some of the common ethical dilemmas that arise in peer support services. We have chosen five 'case studies' from our experience that can be used to think about these issues. As they are presented in Exercise 9.3, they are for managers/supervisors of peer support services to use in thinking about how they would handle these issues in supervision. However, with only minor changes, they can be given to peer supporters to help them think about ethical dilemmas they may encounter. They can be worked on individually or in groups. For group discussion, we suggest using the format detailed in Exercise 8.1.

The second area of supervision knowledge and skill is recognizing and dealing with common problems brought by peer supporters to supervision. Exercise 9.4 offers a format for developing this aspect of supervision.

Finally, it is useful to practise recognizing and dealing with some of the common styles of communication and presentation found in peer support supervision. Exercise 9.5 provides a format for practising this area of skill.

A final word about supervision in the context of peer support

Regular supervision needs to be one of the cornerstones of your peer support service. It will ensure the safety of the young people who use the service and those who work as peer supporters. It can provide many opportunities for emotional growth and skills development for you, the supervisor, and your peer supporters. It can also be tremendous fun, which may be enough reward in itself. It will certainly take some work to develop these skills, but as they can be generalized to a range of settings, we believe you will find it worth the investment personally, and in terms of the success of your peer support service.

Exercise 9.1 *Structuring an individual supervision session*

You have 16 peer supporters to supervise and you have decided to see them individually. You have a maximum of two hours each week in which to do this.

- How frequently will you see each of them?
- How long will each supervision session last?
- How will you ensure that the focus remains on issues that it is necessary to address in supervision? (Remember the functions your supervision needs to perform.)
- Would you do it differently if you had only 8 peer supporters to supervise?

Exercise 9.2 *Structuring a group supervision session*

You have 16 peer supporters to supervise and you have decided to offer group supervision. You have a maximum of two hours free each week in which to do this.

- Will you see all of the peer supporters in one group? If not, how many groups will you have?
- How long will the group supervision sessions be?
- How will you structure the time in the group to ensure that anyone who has a serious concern can raise it but everyone feels they have had their needs attended to?
- Would you do it differently if you had only eight peer supporters to supervise?

Exercise 9.3 *Ethical issues in peer support supervision*

Questions to ask of each case study

- What are the ethical issues raised by this situation?
- What, if any, are the legal issues?
- Are there ways in which the difficulties could have been prevented?
- What will you say to the peer supporter?
- What action will you expect the peer supporter to take?
- What action, if any, will you take?
- What are the possible consequences of these actions?

Case Study I: Gemma

Gemma, one of your peer supporters, comes to see you, saying that she is very concerned about a girl who came to her for peer support. The girl is 14 years old and says she is having a lot of problems at home. Yesterday, she told Gemma that there is something she has never told anyone because she is too ashamed but that she wants to talk to her about it because she trusts her. The girl then asked Gemma to promise that she would not tell anyone about the secret and Gemma agreed.

In addition to the questions above, ask yourself first:

What might the secret be?

Discussion of Case Study I: Gemma

The secret *might* be something serious such as sexual or other abuse, and if you are in a statutory organization such as a school, you will be obliged under the Children Act 1989 to discuss the situation with social services. Many other organizations dealing with young people also follow this policy, although they are not obliged to do so by law. Whatever your policy, Gemma should never have promised to keep a secret without knowing what the secret was. Therefore, Gemma will

continued . . .

need to go back to the girl and explain that if she tells her something that indicates risk to herself or others, Gemma will need to tell you, her supervisor. It is possible that the girl will feel betrayed or misled and not disclose whatever she had intended. It is also possible that the peer support service will get an unwelcome reputation for not keeping confidentiality.

In fact, the likelihood is that the secret is something much less serious than abuse and will need no intervention from an adult. Unfortunately, your peer supporter has put you in a situation where you have to behave as if it is serious until told otherwise.

Case Study 2: Luke

In one of your group supervision sessions for peer supporters, one of the peer supporters, Luke, talks about two people he is supporting. One is a girl who came to him for support about bullying and who now wants to talk to him almost every day at school, and the other is a girl whose mother has just died who prefers to ring him at home. Luke says that this is not a problem for him as he likes to help people. In fact, he presents it as a demonstration that he is a good peer sup-porter. From Luke's account, it *does* appear that these young people are finding the contact helpful.

In addition to the questions above, ask yourself:

What do you think is behind Luke's actions?

How and when will you talk to Luke about this – now, in the group or individually, after the group?

Discussion of Case Study 2: Luke

Luke is over-involved with the girls he is helping and appears to be meeting his own self-esteem needs through feeling needed. He may also be abusing his position as peer supporter to have more intimacy with girls he is attracted to. In either case, he needs to adhere to the boundary rules of the service. You need to reiterate these rules and help Luke decide how he will explain them to the girls he is supporting in a way that is firm but not rejecting. You will need to check that he has done this. Luke will need to look at why he agreed to arrange-ments that he knew were against the boundary rules. He may need help negotiating out of a support relationship with one of the girls so that he is free to establish a friendship with her. As these are sensitive issues to address, it may be best to indicate your disagreement in the group but discuss it in detail with Luke on his own, immediately after the supervision group.

Case Study 3: Kelly

Kelly, a peer supporter, who has arranged to see you urgently, tells you that she is concerned about a 16-year old boy who has been talking to her. She approached him a few weeks ago because he is new in school and she could see that he didn't really fit in. He was always standing on his own and looked generally unhappy. He told her that he is usually on his own at home because his father left when he was young and his mother is always out with men. When he spoke to her yesterday, he said that he wanted to kill himself because no-one cared what happened to him anyway. At the time, Kelly didn't take it too seriously and just said to him that she liked him and that she wouldn't want him to kill himself. But afterwards, she thought about it and decided she should tell you as the peer support supervisor. The boy does not know that she is speaking to you.

Discussion of Case Study 3: Kelly

Kelly is right to come to you as the boy may be serious about killing himself. It would have been better if she had picked that up at the time and suggested he or she talk to you about it. However, she handled it reasonably well in that she expressed concern about him. She will need to look for him very soon (that day or the next at the latest) and tell him that she spoke to you because she was seriously concerned. She will need to ask him to speak to you, and if you feel he is at risk you will need to speak to his GP quickly about a psychiatric referral. (You are obliged under all three Acts to do this.) If he does not come to see you, you must seek him out. And if by any chance he is not at school the next day, then he should be followed up at home. It is possible that the boy will be angry with Kelly and feel she has betrayed his trust. However, it is just as likely that he will feel cared for and appreciate it.

Case Study 4: Lisa

In a group supervision session, Lisa mentions that a girl of 15 has come to see her, saying that she is pregnant and has decided to have an abortion. The girl won't tell her parents because her mother already has enough problems as she is beaten by the girl's father. The girl says that her father would 'kill her' if he found out about her pregnancy. The girl has asked Lisa to come with her when she goes for her appointment at the pregnancy advisory service, but Lisa does not want to go. She is not even sure she agrees with abortion in the first place, but has not said that to the girl. Lisa has been worried about this for a few days, but decided to wait for the supervision group to discuss it as the girl's appointment is not until next week.

Discussion of Case Study 4: Lisa

Lisa should really have come to you about this before the next supervision since she is out of her depth. You need to clarify this with the group. However, she has handled the situation well to date, particularly in keeping her own views to herself. Lisa should not go to the clinic with the girl as it is too much to ask of a peer supporter and it implies the school/organization's support for her action. The girl may well choose to go herself and the clinic may well agree to give her a termination without parental consent, given her social circumstances. Whether or not you feel you need to intervene may depend upon your own views and your organization's policies. One solution would be simply to allow the girl to carry on without Lisa's involvement and say nothing. Another would be to talk to her yourself and offer to find her professional support. Another would be to talk to her and say that you will need to inform her parents. However, in making this decision, you should take seriously her concerns about her father hurting her if he finds out.

Case Study 5: Daniel

In a supervision group, one of your peer supporters, Daniel, talks about his work with a boy who is being bullied. Daniel is visibly angry about this boy's treatment at the hands of another boy. The boy tells him that the bully is constantly taunting him and pushing him around at break time. He has stolen the boy's money and threatens to hurt him if he doesn't give more money next time. Daniel says that the boy he is supporting is too afraid to stand up to the bully and so he, Daniel, is going to confront the bully himself, and 'teach him a lesson'. Daniel is an older and bigger boy than the bully and says he won't have any trouble showing the bully 'who is boss'. Daniel has already had 'a few words' with the bully and told him that he's going to 'sort him out'. The other members of the group know this bully too and support Daniel's plan.

In addition to the questions above, ask yourself:

How and when will you talk to Daniel about this – now, in the group or individually, after the group?

Discussion of Case Study 5: Daniel

Daniel needs to be stopped now and you must make it absolutely clear in the supervision group that no peer supporter should ever resort to bullying, no matter how just the cause. One reason why the peer supporters may be resorting to this is because the bullying is not being addressed any other way. At this point, there are two options: either Daniel needs to tell you who the bully is, then tell the boy who is being bullied that you are now handling the situation and you need to intervene; or, if it has not gone too far, you might consider working with Daniel and the other peer supporters and seeing if they could use conflict-resolutions skills with the bully and the victim to come to a resolution of the problem. You need to monitor this closely.

Exercise 9.4 *Common problems brought to supervision*

Purpose
To increase awareness of the common problems brought by peer supporters to supervision.
To think in advance about ways of dealing with these problems.
To practise dealing with these common problems through role-play (pair or group format).

Procedure
This has been designed as a group training exercise, but can be done in pairs or individually. If you are working on your own, then you can simply go through the scenarios and ask yourself how you would address them within your supervision context. If you are working with a partner, then each of you could alternate playing one of the peer supporters described in the 'problem cards' and the other could practise supervising them on the issue presented. If you have the advantage of a group of at least four people to practise with, then this exercise can be done in its most challenging group format.

Group format
One group member should volunteer to be the 'supervisor' and the rest will be peer supporters.
Each peer supporter selects, without looking, a 'problem card'. Ideally, the 'supervisor' should not see the problems in advance.
Each 'peer supporter' then must present this problem in the mock supervision session and the supervisor must run the supervision group in a way that addresses the issues raised.
This should take less time than a usual supervision – 20–30 minutes is usually enough.
Following debriefing, roles can be changed to allow someone else to act as 'supervisor'. New problems from the groups' own experience can be introduced to keep the situation challenging.

Debriefing
Debriefing should begin with the 'supervisor' saying how s/he felt about her handling of the 'supervision group'.

Whether done in pairs or in the group format, 'peer supporters' can then give the 'supervisor' feedback on how they felt s/he handled their feelings and their problem.

To finish, pairs or the group can then discuss alternative ways of handling the issues and the feelings raised.

Problem cards

No clients

You are rather discouraged because no-one has asked to see you for peer support and the programme has been running for six weeks. Although you know that uptake has been slow in general, some peer supporters have seen 'clients' and you are worried that maybe there is something about you that makes people not want to talk to you. You are rather embarrassed that this might be the case and are therefore nervous about raising it in the supervision group.

Self-disclosure

A boy has come to you for peer support and his problem is that his father has left home because his mother is an alcoholic. He is always arguing with your 'client' and your 'client' has to take a lot of responsibility for his younger siblings. Your 'client' wants his mother to go to the GP to get help with her drinking because she did that once before and was much better for a year or so. Your own family situation is similar, except that your father is now a 'recovering alcoholic' and so you think you can understand your 'client's' situation and you know of a possible solution. You do not know whether you should tell him about your experience, because you have not told other people at the school and also because you don't know if it will help. You are coming to supervision wanting an answer to this dilemma, but also anxious because asking will involve disclosing something about your own family situation.

Coping with emotion and attraction

Someone whom you fancy has come to you for support about some problems he is having with his friends. While you are talking, he starts to get upset and then cries. You feel awkward as you don't know whether and how to comfort him. This is made more uncomfortable by your feelings of attraction to him. You end up putting an arm around him, but you are not sure that is right. You are afraid to raise it in supervision because you are embarrassed to talk about your feelings for your 'client' in case your supervisor thinks you have abused your position as a peer supporter.

Knowing what to do with information
Your 'client' has been talking to you for some time about a bully who has been forcing her to give him her bus money every day. She says this bully has also been threatening other people. Until today, she would not tell you who the bully was in case you told a teacher and then the bully might know that it was she who told. However, yesterday, she told you the bully's name but asked you to keep it a secret. At the time you agreed, but now you are unsure whether or not you should tell your supervisor. You don't want this girl to be hurt by the bully, but you also want someone to stop him.

A problem with no solution
Someone is coming to you for peer support about her sister who is dying of leukaemia. She is always terribly distressed and says she just doesn't want it to happen. You feel helpless because there is nothing you can do to change the situation and each time you see your 'client' she is more upset. You are wondering whether you should ask another peer supporter who is better than you to see your 'client' because you don't think you are helping.

Exercise 9.5 *Styles of presentation and communication*

Purpose
To increase awareness of the common presentations of peer supporters in supervision.
To think in advance about ways of dealing with these presentations.
To practise dealing with these common presentations through role-play (pair or group format).

Procedure
This exercise can be done using any of the formats described for Exercise 9.4. It is most fun when it is acted out in the group format. To make a more complex (and highly entertaining!) exercise, the two sets of cards (9.4 problem cards and 9.5 presentation style cards) can be combined in one group 'supervision'.

Debriefing
This can be done in the same format as described in Exercise 9.4.

Presentation cards

The silent type
Don't offer anything without being asked.
If you are asked how things are going, say: 'OK' and don't elaborate.
If asked to talk about someone you have been supporting, give only one
or two sentences with as little information as possible.
Alternate between looking bored and engaged while other people talk,
but don't be overtly disruptive.
Be aware of the behaviours of other group members and be prepared
to talk about this if asked – being silent does give you time to observe
accurately!

The advice-giver (also known as 'the know-it-all')
Talk about the people you are supporting by saying something like:
'Well, I told her that she needs to think about what she wants. She has
to learn to be more confident and tell people what she thinks.'
In the supervision session, be quick to offer advice to other group
members – 'I wouldn't do it that way. I think you should . . . '
Some of the advice you give can be useful, but present it in a way that
is difficult for others to accept.

The compulsive talker
Always be the first to offer to talk about your work, but make sure you
add in lots of extraneous detail so that the listeners cannot get the
point, if there is one.
Don't pause for breath long enough to let the supervisor intervene,
and if s/he tries, just keep on talking over him/her.
In amongst all the detail, you are probably doing some useful work, but
don't make it easy to get to it.

The compulsive helper
You are sure that everyone needs more help than you, and so, if asked,
say that you are not having any problems at all but you would like to
hear from 'the silent type' as you are worried about him/her.
Try to help the supervisor by encouraging other members if they speak
and tell them how well they are doing even if they are not.
When you talk about your support work, talk about how much your
'client' finds you helpful and how you telephone him/her at home now
'just to see how s/he is getting on'.

The good-enough peer supporter
Offer some information about your peer support work when asked
and give more relevant detail if requested.
Admit that you are finding a particular person or problem difficult to
deal with and look for help with this.
Ask other people about their work in a relatively non-judgemental way.
If you have an idea that might help someone else, offer it tentatively.

10

EVALUATION

Why evaluate?

In order to gain recognition for the worth of an intervention, you will often be asked to provide evidence about the quality of your intervention. It is our view that once you engage regularly in the activity of evaluation, you will find that it enhances your practice. As innovators, you can then engage with increasing confidence in the task of developing ideas, putting them into practice, measuring the impact of these practices on users and supporters and the organization, reflecting on the outcomes of your evaluation, and changing the practices in the light of these reflections.

When embarking on an evaluation, particularly in the type of 'real-world' investigation of peer support systems, it is important to pay attention to a range of perspectives on the context of peer support (see Cowie and Sharp, 1996, Chapter 11 for a list of useful measures of peer support). Aspects of peer support to be evaluated are likely to include:

- the judgements of users and potential users of the system;
- the experiences of the peer supporters themselves;
- changes in the climate or ethos of the organization as demonstrated through participants' behaviour or through trends in performance indicators, such as absence rates;
- interpersonal processes in which participants engage.

The first step in evaluating the impact of an intervention such as peer support is to identify the area that is to be the focus of the research. The questions that you will wish to ask at this stage may include:

- **What is the nature of the peer support we plan to introduce?**
- **What do I want to measure?**
- **What is my starting-point? What baseline measures do we need to make?**
- **Where, if at all, do we expect change to have taken place?**

- Why, if at all, has this change occurred?
- How, if at all, has my intervention worked?
- What are the characteristics of the effective peer supporter?
- How can we create a facilitating environment for peer support?
- What improvements do we need to make?

It will be useful at this stage to make contact with some other organizations that are in process of carrying out similar evaluations. By networking, you will gain ideas on the range of measures available, you can share your own expertise and experience, and you can identify new research questions as they emerge.

Independent studies of peer support complement the observations of practitioners. In these studies, we can also identify a range of aspects that lend themselves to evaluation. We begin with examples of baseline measures that give helpful information on the changes that take place over time before and after the introduction of an intervention such as peer support. We also look at examples of peer support evaluations of the impact on *user satisfaction*, on *peer supporters*, and on the *organization as a whole*. In each study, we provide an example of the measure that was used. You can adapt these measures to the requirements of the peer support system that you would like to evaluate.

The effect of peer mediation on behaviour in the playground

In a Canadian study of the effects of student-mediated conflict resolution in primary school, Cunningham et al. (1998) found that, over time, interventions of this type improved the social climate of a school and significantly reduced physical aggression during break-times. Cunningham and his colleagues used observational methods at three time-points – before the intervention, during the intervention and at a follow-up – to evaluate the effect of introducing a peer mediation service into three primary schools. The repeated weekly observations provided information about the impact of the programme on children's behaviour in the playground (Box 10.1).

Mediators also carried a clipboard with a prompt sheet for examples of behaviours that warranted or did not require intervention. For each conflict in which they intervened, mediators recorded the gender and grade of the disputants, the nature of the conflict (*physical* versus *verbal/relational*), and whether the conflict was resolved successfully. Mediators coded *physical* conflict when disputants engaged in aggressive behaviour with physical contact, for example pushing, kicking or hitting. *Verbal/relational* conflict referred to aggressive behaviours such as nasty teasing of another person or social exclusion. Mediation was judged successful if: (a) both disputants agreed to mediate in the conflict; (b) a solution was agreed on; (c) the mediator felt the solution solved the problem.

Box 10.1 *Direct observation of student behaviour in the playground (adapted from Cunningham et al., 1998, pp. 655–7)*

A team of three coders conducted observations once weekly during two 20-minute recess (break) periods, with one observer assigned to each of three schools. In general, observations were conducted at the same time, from the same location, by the same observer. The following behaviours were recorded at regular intervals:

Physical aggression. This category included instances of physical aggression, such as taking equipment from peers, pushing another student, or hitting.

Adult intervention. Instances in which adults intervened to prevent or resolve conflicts.

On the basis of the observations, the authors were able to conclude that the introduction of the mediation scheme resulted in a sustained drop in aggressive behaviour in the playground (Figure 10.1).

Aggressive incidents decreased (from an average in one of the schools of 57 per cent to 28 per cent) during mediation. These effects were still evident during the follow-up period. The mediator monitoring records

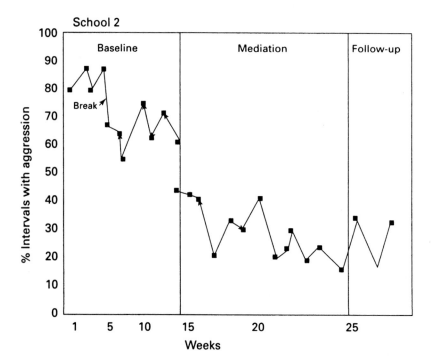

Figure 10.1 *Playground observation during baseline, mediation and follow-up*

confirmed that students co-operated with the mediation team. In fact, all of the schools in the study selected and trained a second generation of mediators in the following year. The mediators detected conflict early and were able to intervene quickly before it escalated. The authors conclude that, as a relatively low-cost intervention, it merits wider use and further study as part of an anti-violence school programme.

Changes in the incidence of bullying behaviour over four time-points

Smith and Sharp (1994) analysed the results from playground monitoring of the effects of anti-bullying interventions in 23 Sheffield schools. They began with baseline measures (short questionnaires) before the intervention was implemented, and then monitored its effect by administering the same questionnaires to certain year-groups each day for one week in each term of the project. The researchers distinguished among different types of bullying: physical, rumour-spreading, name-calling, threatening behaviour, social exclusion, stealing belongings and racist name-calling. The results as shown in Figure 10.2 show a substantial reduction in all types of bullying.

An average reduction of 46 per cent occurred between the first monitoring in November 1991 and the fourth in November 1992. By gathering these data, the researchers were able to pinpoint when the changes

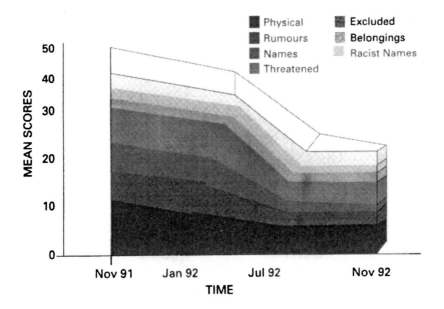

Figure 10.2 *Rates of bullying at four time-points*

occurred. The biggest positive change took place between the latter part of the spring term and the first half of the summer term when the newly developed whole school anti-bullying policies were being most actively implemented. As a confirmation of this interpretation of the results, it was found that in the school that was least active in the development and implementation of the intervention, there was an increase in bullying during this period.

Bubble dialogue 'comic-strip' technique

Bubble dialogue is a technique for eliciting perceptions of what another person might be thinking but not saying (Naylor, 1999). Participants are presented with a comic-strip story containing spoken dialogue and asked to imagine what the characters in each scene are thinking at that moment. Empty 'think' bubbles are provided for the respondents to complete, so encouraging them to imagine the private worlds of the characters in the comic strip. The method can be used as part of a need analysis or as an evaluation before and after the introduction of a peer support system.

In Figure 10.3 (one panel from a story) we see how the technique can reveal what a person imagines others might be thinking, for example when one intervenes to help the victim of racist bullying. Here the participants have the chance to write in the 'think' bubbles what Choi, Rebecca and

Figure 10.3 *Bubble dialogue*

another peer may be thinking when the teacher insists that Choi lends her rubber to Rebecca and ignores the racist name-calling.

The advantage of this method is that it gives participants the opportunity to take the role of different people in a bullying situation, in the sense that it is the comic-strip characters who speak and think. This means that the participants who construct the dialogue are free of the constraints that they might feel in a real-life situation. Furthermore, the method is accessible, does not require a high level of literacy, and is quick to administer.

Who are peer supporters and why do they volunteer?

The Mental Health Foundation funded five inner-city schools to set up peer support projects to promote the mental health of their students. The project team carried out some baseline measures before the training of peer supporters took place. One aim of this study (Rogers et al., 1999) was to obtain demographic information on the peer supporters, to establish the views and aspirations of these students as they embarked on the project, and to consider their motivation for taking part. The measure used was a questionnaire that consisted of a series of structured and open-ended questions (see Box 10.2). Ninety-nine peer supporters completed the questionnaires.

The peer supporters gave a number of reasons for wishing to take part in the programme:

- Eighty-one per cent wanted to help other students to know where to turn to for support.
- Eighty-one per cent stated that they wanted other students to know that it is OK to ask for help.
- Seventy-five per cent reported that they wanted to make a positive contribution to the school community.
- Sixty-eight per cent reported that they wanted to help their peers.

Note that since peer supporters could give more than one reason for wishing to take part, the total is more than 100 per cent.

Participant Role Scales

The Participant Role Scales devised by Salmivalli et al. (1996) are a series of statements describing pupil behaviour in bullying situations in a number of participant roles. These roles are as follows:

- **bully** – leading and initiating bullying behaviour; actively involved in bullying;

Box 10.2 *Demographic information on peer supporters (adapted from Rogers et al., 1999)*

---

1. Name
2. Date
3. Name of school/FE college/club
4. Year-group
5. Gender
6. Please tick the circle below which best describes your ethnic origin

Bangladeshi	○
Black African-Caribbean	○
Black African	○
Black other (please specify)	○
Chinese	○
Indian	○
Irish	○
Pakistani	○
White	○
White – other (please specify)	○
Other (please specify)	○

The information gathered from this part of the survey was as follows:
Eighty-one per cent of peer supporters were female.
The ethnic origins of peer supporters were varied, with 39 per cent White and 61 per cent from minority groups.
Peer supporters ranged in age from 11 to 17 years.
Forty per cent of the peer supporters were from year-group 12, that is, were 16 years old.

- **assistant to the bully** – supporting the bully; eagerly joining in the bullying;
- **reinforcer** – acting as an audience; laughing at the victim; encouraging the behaviour of the bully;
- **victim** – the target of bullying behaviour;
- **defender** – providing direct or indirect support to the victimized person; trying to stop the bullying by, for example, telling an adult or telling the others to stop; comforting the victim after the event;
- **outsider** – ignoring or avoiding bullying situations; pretending not to notice that bullying is taking place.

The original Participant Role Scale (PRS) was designed for use with individual secondary-aged pupils. Later, it was revised for group administration. Sutton and Smith (1999) have adapted the scales for use with individual younger pupils. For the full version of the PRS for older pupils and group administration, and for younger pupils and individual administration, with precise scoring instructions, see Sharp (1999). We present some examples of items for each participant role scale in Box 10.3. These questions can be administered to a whole class.

The ratings (score 1 for 'they only do it sometimes', score 2 for 'they do it a lot') assigned to each pupil for each scale by all the pupils in a class are added together to give a total score. If a person has been nominated as being in a particular role by more than 30 per cent of peers, then they are assigned to that role.

The value of the PRS is that it is possible to map out the bullying relationships in the whole social context of the class-group. In Table 10.1,

Box 10.3 *Participant Role Scales (adapted from Sutton and Smith, 1999)*

Bully Scale
  1. Which boys or girls lead a gang that bullies others?
  2. Which boys or girls do mean things to others, like picking on them, hitting them or pushing them?

Assistant to the Bully Scale
  3. Which boys or girls join in the bullying when someone else has started it?
  4. Which boys or girls help the bully, maybe by catching or holding the victim?

Reinforcer Scale
  5. Which boys or girls encourage the bully by shouting?
  6. Which boys or girls say things to the bully like 'Show him/her!'

Victim Scale
  7. Which boys or girls get bullied by others?
  8. Which boys or girls get called nasty names among your classmates?

Defender Scale
  9. Which boys or girls tell an adult about the bullying?
  10. Which boys or girls try to cheer the victim up?

Outsider Scale
  11. Which boys or girls pretend not to notice what is happening when someone is being bullied?
  12. Which boys or girls do not even notice that the bullying is going on?

Table 10.1 *The percentage of children and adolescents in the different participant roles in sixth (n = 573) and eighth (n = 316) grades*

Participant role	Sixth grade	Eighth grade
Victim	12	6
Bully	8	9
Assistant to the bully	7	11
Reinforcer of the bully	19	15
Outsider	24	32
Defender of the victim	17	19
No clear role	13	8
Total	100	100

Source: Adapted from Salmivalli, 1999

you can see that most students act in ways that maintain or even encourage bullying rather than diminish it, despite the fact that most young people report that they are against bullying (Whitney and Smith, 1993). Unfortunately, in the context of a group of peers, there can be pressures to conform to certain behaviours which may not always be pro-social.

Salmivalli found that 17 per cent of grade 6 (age 10) and 19 per cent of grade 8 (age 12) pupils were nominated to the defender role. She also points out that defenders have high status among their peers and tend to have high self-esteem and a positive image of themselves (Salmivalli et al., 1999). However, in schools with a peer support system in place, you could predict that this percentage would increase. The PRS could therefore make a useful baseline measure before a peer support intervention was put in place. Salmivalli's (1999) findings support the idea of targeting the whole class-group rather than simply concentrating on the bully and the victim when trying to change the quality of young people's social relationships.

The benefits experienced by peer supporters

Cowie (1998) conducted interviews in nine schools in the UK, two primary and seven secondary, where peer support systems had been well established for at least one year (range 1–4 years, mean length of time 2.4 years) as part of a school anti-bullying policy. The systems included: informal *befriending schemes*, where peer supporters were trained to offer friendship or support in everyday interaction with peers; a *conflict-resolution scheme*, where peer supporters were trained to work through a process of mediation in order to address common interpersonal problems in the school, such as bullying, racist name-calling, fighting and exclusion; and *counselling-based schemes*, where support took place in specially designated rooms, usually through a system of appointments and over a period of time. In the latter, supervision by an adult with training in counselling occurred at regular times.

Box 10.4 *Interviews with peer supporters and teachers about benefits and problems (adapted from Cowie, 1998)*

- What are the perceived benefits of your peer support scheme for the peer helpers?
- What are the perceived benefits of your peer support scheme for the school as a whole?
- What problems, if any, have you encountered?
- Are there any ways in which the service could be improved?

All the schools in the study offered peer support to pupils affected by bullying; invited applications from potential helpers from all pupils within a given age-group, usually but not always older pupils; provided training in the skills of active, empathic listening; prepared the helpers to be sensitive to behavioural signs of distress in the peer group; and were committed to a person-centred, no-blame perspective. All provided support to the helpers through regular opportunities for debriefing or supervision. Teachers and peer helpers were asked the questions in Box 10.4.

Without exception, all peer helpers reported that there were great personal benefits for them through their involvement in the scheme. Sixty per cent reported that these benefits arose directly from the interpersonal skills and teamwork acquired in the course of training. In other words, the most frequently mentioned advantages were that they experienced an increase in self-confidence, a sense of responsibility and a belief that they were contributing positively to the life of the school community.

These enhanced personal qualities seemed to arise from a number of sources. The majority of the peer helpers (63 per cent) expressed the belief that the service was having an impact on the school as a whole. Others reported their perception that school was becoming a place where it was more acceptable to talk about emotional and relationship issues. The adults in charge of the schemes were unanimous in confirming that the work of the peer support service went far beyond the help offered to individuals in need – valuable as that was seen to be – and that it affected the whole school. Peer supporters in this study reported that they appreciated the opportunity of addressing a real problem in their school community and being given the skills and structures to tackle it. Peer supporters commented favourably on the usefulness of the communication skills that they learned in the course of training. Such 'empowerment' of young people was perceived in a positive light by the teachers in charge of the service, though less so by other uninvolved colleagues.

The impact of training on peer educators

Peer education is another area where young people themselves have a part to play in disseminating information to the peer group on sexual behaviour, alcohol use and issues around drugs, as Elliott and Lambourn (1999) showed in their study of peer education in the bicultural context of Aotearoa or New Zealand, where Maori and Pacific Island New Zealanders are over-represented in statistics on illiteracy, neonatal death, lung cancer, teenage pregnancy, smoking and crime. Young peer educators were given Peer Sexuality Support (PSS) training. They learned, amongst other things, to make constructive use of the cultural traditions of Aotearoa by incorporating democratic discussion groups to explore ways of disseminating information in a culturally sensitive way.

Elliott and Lambourn used focus groups (Box 10.5) to find out how the young peer educators had experienced the training.

The programme was highly valued by the peer educators and to some it was 'a life-changing experience'. Others reported heightened self-esteem and self-confidence and increased motivation to help others. They also reported: clarity in identifying their own values with respect to sexual choices:

> It has made me more confident and a little wiser.

> I now realize how lucky I am to be who I am rather than wanting to be someone else.

> It has enlightened me to think of others more deeply and to care for myself to a deeper extent.

The focus group discussions revealed that problems with the system were: 'opposition to discussion of sexuality and sexual health by fundamentalist groups'; and 'some difficulties in school support on the part of staff not involved in peer education'.

The perspective of users of a peer support service

As part of a survey carried out in 51 secondary schools with an established peer support system in place, Naylor and Cowie (1999) elicited the views of 65 users of the schemes in two year-groups (Box 10.6).

Of the 65 pupil users of their school's peer support system who responded to the question about how helpful they found it, 82 per cent responded 'very helpful' or 'helpful' and 18 per cent 'not helpful'. The three most commonly mentioned benefits for users were that the service provides 'somebody to talk to and who listens', 'the strength to overcome the problem' and that it 'shows that somebody cares'.

In answer to the question 'please say what you think the benefits of peer support are', those most frequently mentioned by peer supporters and

Box 10.5 *The use of focus groups as an evaluation tool (adapted from Elliott and Lambourn, 1999)*

The technique of interviewing participants in focus groups is widely used in marketing research as an exploratory research method to help companies gain a deeper understanding of their customers' percep-tions, feelings, motivations and desires, but it is also used successfully with young people to elicit their views in a safe environment. Focus groups are a well-respected means of gathering in-depth, qualitative information about opinions and attitudes on a wide range of issues.

Focus groups typically bring 8 to 12 people (adults or young people) together for a round-table discussion. The participants are selected because they share certain characteristics (for example, that they are peer supporters, or users, or potential users, or teachers in charge of the system) that are relevant to the study.

The interviewer creates a permissive environment, and asks focused questions to encourage discussion and the expression of differing points of view. Participants are given the opportunity to listen to one another's point of view. The interviewer must be skilled in eliciting the participants' self-disclosure through the creation of a permissive environment. The format allows the exploration of unanticipated issues as they arise in the discussion. A number of techniques may be used to elicit the participants' ideas and experi-ences, including facilitating questions (for example, asking for clarification of an opinion offered by a participant), and vignettes (for example, experiences of young people in other social settings, such as youth clubs).

Focus group sessions are usually recorded by video- or audio-tape for further analysis. As a rule, a number of sessions with different groups will be conducted in a well-designed focus group project. This not only ensures confidentiality and eliminates bias, but also provides valuable information through allowing comparisons between groups.

The focus group method allows scope for the authentic voices of respondents and gives the researcher an opportunity to hear the stories that emanate from a group. Focus groups encourage open discussion of sensitive issues, for example about sexual behaviour. They enable the researcher to probe for meanings that might otherwise be unspoken.

teachers concerned the acquisition and development of skills and being in a 'caring school'. The three most frequently mentioned benefits of a peer support system to the school as a whole were that 'the school cares', 'bullying is reduced' and 'teachers are freed to do other things'. The idea of a caring school was mentioned by over 40 per cent of the users of these systems.

Box 10.6 *Perspectives of peer supporters (adapted from Naylor and Cowie, 1999)*

Have you ever used your school's peer support service?   YES   NO

If YES, please say how helpful it was:

Very helpful   Helpful   Not helpful

Please describe your most helpful experience of peer support

....

....

....

....

Please describe your least helpful experience of peer support

....

....

....

....

Are there any ways in which the peer support service could be improved?

....

....

....

....

Please say what you think the benefits of peer support are to:

(a) users ....

(b) peer supporters ....

(c) the school ....

The wider survey also indicated that the existence of a peer support system was perceived as beneficial to the school as a whole. Many pupils who had not used the system still appreciated the provision of a service to protect their safety, and viewed its presence as a sign that the school was caring.

Perceptions by users of a befriending service

Abu-Rasain and Williams (1999) describe the positive impact of a befriending peer support service on peer relationships among the boys in a secondary school in Saudi Arabia, even though, as the authors point out, the ethos of counselling-based support is quite alien to the kingdom's culture. To measure client satisfaction, the researchers interviewed 66 users in confidence about the issues shown in Box 10.7.

Box 10.7 *Users' questionnaire (adapted from Abu-Rasain and Williams, 1999)*

- How often did you meet with your peer supporter?
- In what ways was peer support helpful to you?
- In what ways was peer support less helpful to you?
- Overall, were you satisfied with the service?
- Would you use it again if you had a problem?
- Would you recommend the service to another person in your school/organization?
- Are there any ways in which the service could be improved?

In this study, the users identified the qualities of 'accepting', 'showing an interest' and 'making me feel safe' as the most helpful aspects of peer support. They also endorsed the value of the service by reporting that the peer supporters 'helped me with my issue' and 'made me feel better'. There was significant satisfaction with the service, and agreement that they would use it again. Dissatisfaction with the service was ascribed to 'lack of teachers' support' and 'needing more time'.

The users reported that they would recommend the service to others in distress because 'it was not embarrassing to talk to a fellow student'. By means of an anonymous questionnaire, the users of the service were able to give invaluable information to the organizer of the peer support service about how well it was working. They also provided some suggestions about how it could work better, for example by:

- the use of equal opportunities principles in recruiting peer supporters;
- developing more positive support from other teachers and the school administration;

- affirmation of the need for peer supporters to be trustworthy and popular;
- provision of training so that peer supporters could be knowledgeable in this field.

Conclusion

In this chapter, we have described some ways in which peer support systems might be evaluated. This is not an exhaustive list but a set of guidelines that you can adapt for your own purposes. Evaluation strategies will vary according to the needs of participants and the communities where peer support takes place. It is our argument, however, that all peer support systems will benefit from an evaluation/monitoring process which is embedded into the system from the beginning. Evaluation is part of a spirit of enquiry that is more effective when there is a climate of trust, a willingness to be open, a genuine concern to be constructively critical and an interest in working co-operatively as part of a team.

We have come full circle in this book. The final chapter of this book is about evaluation, but we do not suggest that this is the end of the story. Rather it could represent a new beginning, as adults and young people reflect on the outcomes and processes of their peer support work, and collaboratively plan new strategies and approaches. As we saw in the introductory chapter, when adults and young people have become accustomed to taking part regularly in a process of observation, analysis and reflection, they have a choice. They may choose to consolidate their peer support system, or they may take the opportunity to renew the cycle by identifying new goals. They can return to the stage of orientation, but from a different perspective and grounded in actual experience (See Figure 0.1), and so the cycle of change continues.

In this book, we have described the establishment of systems of peer support in schools and in other organizations concerned with youth. It is our belief that peer support systems give valuable opportunities for bystanders to act in defence of vulnerable peers, and so create contexts that are safer from violence and aggression. At the heart of the approach that we have offered here is a commitment to positive relationships and a concern for the self-esteem of younger people. Peer support systems also offer the opportunity for adults to reconsider their own ways of relating to the young people in their charge and to one another and to reflect on the messages that they are conveying in their everyday interactions.

We believe that it is possible to create environments that promote rather than discourage pro-social ways of living and communicating with others. Peer support is one strand in the education of our future citizens. It is our belief that through the experience of peer support in action children and young people can develop the knowledge, skills and understandings that they will need as they face the roles and responsibilities of adult life. It is our hope that the book will provide a resource for practitioners who are committed, as we are, to developing positive relationships and supporting pro-social environments for children and young people.

REFERENCES

Aboud, F. (1988) *Children and Prejudice*. Oxford: Blackwell.

Abu-Rasain, M.H.M. and Williams, D. (1999) Peer counselling in Saudi Arabia. *Journal of Adolescence*, 22, 493–502.

Acland, A.F. (1990) *A Sudden Outbreak of Common Sense: Managing Conflict through Mediation*. London: Hutchinson Business Books.

Acland, A.F. (1997) Paper presented at the Mediation Mid-Wales Conference on 14 March 1997. Available from Mediation UK, Alexander House, Telephone Avenue, Bristol, BS1 4BS, UK.

Acton, A. (1989) Democratic practice in a primary school. In C. Harber and R. Meighan (eds), *The Democratic School: Education Management and the Practice of Democracy*. Ticknall: Education Now Publishing Cooperative.

Adler, P.S. (1987) Is ADR a Social Movement? *Negotiation Journal*, 3(1), 59–71.

Advisory Group on Citizenship (1998) *Education for Citizenship and Teaching of Democracy in Schools (The Crick Report)*. London: QCA.

Andrews, S. (1989) The ignominy of raised hands. In C. Harber and R. Meighan (eds) *The Democratic School: Education Management and the Practice of Democracy*. Ticknall: Education Now Publishing Cooperative.

BAC (1994) *Counselling, Confidentiality and the Law*. Rugby: British Association for Counselling.

BAC (1997) *Code of Ethics and Practice for Counsellors*. Rugby: British Association for Counselling.

Barnes, D. (1984) *From Communication to Curriculum*. London: Penguin.

Beer, J., Steif, E. and Walker, C. (1987) *Peacemaking in Your Neighborhood: Mediator's Handbook*. Concordville, PA: Friends Suburban Project.

Bennett, M. and Dunne, E. (1992) *Managing Classroom Groups*. Hemel Hempstead: Simon and Schuster.

Björkqvist, K. and Fry, D. (1997) Conclusions: alternatives to violence. In D. Fry and K. Björkqvist (eds), *Cultural Variation in Conflict Resolution*, Mahwah, NJ: Lawrence Erlbaum Associates.

Bliss, T. and Tetley, J. (1997) *Circle Time*. Bristol: Lucky Duck Publishing.

Bobbett, P. (1996) *Children Working for Peace*. Oxford: Unicef.

Bond, T. (1993) *Standards and Ethics for Counselling in Action*. London: Sage.

Boulding, K.E. (1962) *Conflict and Defence: A General Theory*. New York and London: Harper and Row.

Boulton, M., Trueman, M., Chau, C., Whiteland, C. and Amatya, K. (1999) Concurrent and longitudinal links between friendship and peer victimization: implications for befriending interventions. *Journal of Adolescence*, 22(4), 461–6.

Brace, A. (1995) Now mediation is the word in the war on school violence. *The Mail on Sunday*, 19 March.

Brandes, D. and Ginnis, P. (1990) *The Student-Centred School*. Oxford: Blackwell.

Burton, J.W. (1990) *Conflict: Resolution and Prevention*. New York: St Martin's Press London: Macmillan.

Cameron, J. and Dupuis, A. (1991) The introduction of school mediation to New Zealand. *Journal of Research and Development in Education*, 24(3), 1–13.

Carroll, M. (1996) *Counselling Supervision: Theory, Skills and Practice*. London: Cassell.

Cartwright, N. (1996) Combating bullying in school: the role of peer helpers. In H. Cowie and S. Sharp (eds), *Peer Counselling in Schools: a Time to Listen*. London: David Fulton Publishers.

Cohen, R. (1995) *Peer Mediation in Schools: Students Resolving Conflict*. Glenview: Goodyear Books.

Cole, T. (1987) *Kids Helping Kids*. University of Victoria, BC.

Cook, S. (1995) Mediation as an alternative to probation revocation proceedings. *Federal Probation*, 59.

Cowie, H. (1998) Perspectives of teachers and pupils on the experience of peer support against bullying. *Educational Research and Evaluation*, 4, 108–25.

Cowie, H. and Olafsson, R. (2000) The role of peer support in helping the victims of bullying in a school with high levels of aggression. *School Psychology International*, 21:1; 79–95.

Cowie, H. and Rudduck, J. (1988) *Co-operative Group Work: an Overview*. London: BP Educational Service.

Cowie, H. and Sharp, S. (eds) (1996) *Peer Counselling in Schools*. London: David Fulton Publishers.

Cowie, H. and van der Aalsvoort, D. (2000) *Social Interaction in Learning and Instruction: the Meaning of Discourse for the Construction of Knowledge*. London: Pergamon Press.

Cowie, H., Smith, P.K., Boulton, M. and Laver, R. (1994) *Co-operation in the Multiethnic Classroom*. London: David Fulton Publishers.

Craig, W. and Pepler, D. (1995) Peer processes in bullying and victimization: an observational study. *Exceptionality Education Canada*, 5, 81–95.

Crary, D.R. (1992) Community benefits from mediation: a test of the 'peace virus' hypothesis. *Mediation Quarterly*, 9(3), 241–52.

CRDU (1994) *UK Agenda for Children*. Children's Rights Development Unit.

Cunningham, C., Cunningham, L., Martorelli, V., Tran, A., Young, J. and Zacharias, R. (1998) The effects of primary division, student-mediated conflict resolution programs on playground aggression. *Journal of Child Psychology and Psychiatry*, 39(5), 653–662.

Daniels, D. and Jenkins, P. (2000) *Therapy with Children*. London: Sage.

Davis, G., Messmar, H., Umbreit, M. and Coates, R. (1992) *Making Amends*. London: Routledge.

de Haan, W. (1990) *The Politics of Redress*. London: Unwin Hyman.

Demetriades, A. (1996) Children of the Storm: peer partnership. In H. Cowie and S. Sharp (eds), *Peer Counselling in Schools: a Time to Listen*. London: David Fulton Publishers.

Deutsch, M. (1973) *The Resolution of Conflict*. New Haven, CT: Yale University Press.

DfEE (1999) *Secondary Schools' Performance Tables 1998*. London: Department for Education and Employment.

Druckman, D. (1977) *Negotiations: Social-Psychological Perspectives*. Beverly Hills, CA: Sage.

Duncan, Y. (1993) *Report on Cool Schools Mediation Programme*. Available from Mediation UK, Alexander House, Telephone Avenue, Bristol, BS1 4BS, UK.

Dunn, J. and Kendrick, C. (1982) *Siblings: Love, Envy and Understanding*. Oxford: Blackwell.

Dunn, J., Brown, J.R. and Beardsall, L. (1991) Family talk about emotions, and children's later understanding of others' emotions. *Developmental Psychology*, 27, 448–55.

Dunne, E. and Bennett, N. (1990) *Talking and Learning in Groups*. London: Macmillan.

Egan, G. (1990) *Exercises in Helping Skills: a Training Manual to Accompany The Skilled Helper*. Pacific Grove, CA: Brooks/Cole Publishing Company.

Egan, G. (1994) *The Skilled Helper: A Problem-management Approach to Helping*. (5th edition). Pacific Grove, CA: Brooks/Cole Publishing Company.

Elliott, K. and Lambourn, A. (1999) Sex, drugs and alcohol: two peer-led approaches in Tamaki Makaurau/Auckland, Aotearoa/New Zealand. *Journal of Adolescence*, 22, 503–513.

ENCORE (1997) *Encore News 1997*. Available from the Education Advisor, Quaker Peace and Service, Friends House, Euston Rd, London, NW12BJ, UK.

Farley-Lucas, B., Tardy, R. and Hale, C.L. (1996) Interpersonal conflict from a younger point of view. *International Journal of Qualitative Studies in Education*, 9(3), 269–91.

Fine, N. and Macbeth, F. (1992a) *Playing with Fire: Training for the Creative Use of Conflict*. Leicester: Youth Work Press.

Fine, N. and Macbeth, F. (1992b) *Fireworks: Creative Approaches to Conflict*. Leicester: Youth Work Press.

Finn, P. (1981) Institutionalizing peer education in the health education classroom. *The Journal of School Health*, 51(2), 91–5.

Fisher, P. and Ury, W. (1981) *Getting to Yes: Negotiating Agreement Without Giving In*. Boston: Houghton Mifflin.

Foot, H. and Howe, C. (1998) The psychoeducational basis of peer-assisted learning. In K. Topping and S. Ehly (eds), *Peer-assisted Learning*. Mahwah, NJ: Lawrence Erlbaum.

Foot, H., Morgan, M. and Shute, R. (eds), (1990) *Children Helping Children*. Chichester: Wiley.

Frisz, R. (1999) Multi-cultural peer counseling: counseling the multicultural student, *Journal of Adolescence*, 22, 515–526.

Fry, D.P. and Björkqvist, K. (eds) (1997) (eds), *Cultural Variation in Conflict Resolution*. Mahwah, NJ: Lawrence Erlbaum.

Fry, D.P. and Fry, C.P. (1997) Culture and conflict-resolution models: exploring alternatives to violence. In D.P. Fry and K. Björkqvist (eds), *Cultural Variation in Conflict Resolution*. Mahwah, NJ: Lawrence Erlbaum.

Galton, M. and Williamson, J. (1992) *Group Work in the Primary Classroom*. London: Routledge.

Gentry, D.B. and Benenson, J.M. (1993) School to home transfer of conflict management skills among school-age children. *Families in Society*, 72(2), 67–73.

Goleman, D. (1996) *Emotional Intelligence*. London: Bloomsbury.

Haigh, G. (1994) Blessed are the peacemakers. *Times Educational Supplement*, 6 October.

Hanko, G. (1999) *Increasing Competence through Collaborative Problem-solving*. London: David Fulton Publishers.

Hawkins, P. and Shohet, R. (1989) *Supervision in the Helping Professions*. Milton Keynes: Open University Press.

Hay, D.G., Zahn-Waxler, C., Cummings, E.M. and Iannotti, R.J. (1992) Young children's views about conflict with peers: a comparison of the daughters and sons of depressed and well women. *Journal of Child Psychology and Psychiatry*, 33, 669–83.

Haynes, J. (1993) *Alternative Dispute Resolution: Fundamentals of Family Mediation.* London: Old Bailey Press.

Hazler, R. (1996) Bystanders: an overlooked factor in peer-on-peer abuse. *The Journal for the Professional Counselor*, 11, 11–21.

Highfield Junior School (1997) *Changing Our School*. London: Institute of Education, University of London.

Horbury, H. and Pears, H. (1994) Collaborative group-work: how infant children can manage it. *Education 3–13*, 22(3), 20–8.

Jaques, D. (1984) *Learning in Groups*. London: Croom Helm.

Jenkins, P. (1997) *Counselling, Psychotherapy and the Law*. London: Sage.

Johnson, D.W. and Johnson, R. (1980) Group processes: Influences of student–student interaction on school outcomes. In J. McMillam (ed.), *The Social Psychology of School Learning*. New York: Academic Press.

Johnson, D.W. and Johnson, R. (1994) Constructive conflict in the schools. *Journal of Social Issues*, 50(1), 117–37.

Johnson, D.W. and Johnson, R. (1996) Conflict resolution and peer mediation programs in elementary and secondary schools: a review of the research. *Review of Educational Research*, 66(4), 459–506.

Johnson, D.W., Johnson, R., Dudley, B. and Acikgoz, K. (1994) Effects of conflict resolution training on elementary school students. *Journal of Social Psychology*, 134(6), 803–17.

Kelly, J. (1990) Is mediation less expensive? Comparison of mediated and adversarial divorce costs. *Mediation Quarterly*, 8(1), 15–26.

Kochenderfer, B. and Ladd, G.L. (1997) Victimised children's responses to peers' aggression: behaviours associated with reduced versus continued victimisation. *Development and Psychopathology*, 9, 59–73.

Kolb, D.A. (1976) Management and the learning process. *California Management Review*, 18(3), 21–31.

Konfliktradet (1999) End of project evaluation of the Asker and Baerum development programme in school mediation. *Peer Support Networker*, 11, 4–5.

Kingston Friends Workshop Group (KFWG) (1988) *Mediation*. Quaker Meeting House, 78 Eden Street, Kingston-upon-Thames, Surrey KT1 1DJ.

Leimdorfer, T. (1990) Teaching creative responses to conflict. *New Era in Education*, 71(2), 54–7.

McMahon, C. (1997) Conflict Resolution Network Schools Australia. *European Journal of Intercultural Studies*, 8(2), 169–84.

McNamara, K. (1996) 'Say NO to bullying!': a message from your peers. *Pastoral Care in Education*, 14(2), 16–20.

Maines, B. and Robinson, G. (1990) *You Can, You Know You Can*. Bristol: Lucky Duck Publishing.

Maines, B. and Robinson, G. (1994) *Managing Children . . . Managing Themselves*. Bristol: Lucky Duck Publishing.

Maresca, J. (1995) Mediating child protection cases. *Child Welfare*, 74, 731–42.

Masheder, M. (1986) *Let's Cooperate: Activities and Ideas for Parents and Teachers of Young Children for Peaceful Conflict Solving*. London: Peace Education Project.

Maslow, A. (1962) *Towards a Psychology of Being*. Princeton, NJ: Van Nostrand.

Mathie, E. and Ford, N. (1998) Peer education for health. In K. Topping and S. Ehly (eds), *Peer-assisted Learning*. Mahwah, NJ: Lawrence Erlbaum.

Miller, R.W. (1993) In search of peace. *Schools in the Middle*, 2(3).

Mosley, J. (1996) *Quality Circle Time in the Primary School*. Wisbech: Learning Development Aids.

National Curriculum Council (1989) *Teaching Talking and Learning in Key Stage Three*. National Curriculum Council, National Oracy Project.

Naylor, P. (1999) Adolescents' conceptions of teacher racism: an investigation using bubble dialogue as a research tool. *Research in Education*, 61, 85–87.

Naylor, P. and Cowie, H. (1998) *The Effectiveness of Peer Support Systems in Challenging School Bullying: The Perspectives and Experiences of Teachers and Pupils*. London: The Prince's Trust.

Naylor, P. and Cowie, H. (1999) The effectiveness of peer support systems in challenging school bullying: the perspectives and experiences of teachers and pupils. *Journal of Adolescence*, 22(4), 1–13.

Nersnæs, L. (1999) A presentation of national actions to prevent school violence. Unpublished paper presented at the First International Forum on Initiatives for Safe School, Seoul, Korea, June.

Newton, C. and Wilson, D. (1999) *Circles of Friends*. Dunstable: Folens.

Nutall, J. (1990) Conflict resolution. *World Studies Journal*, 8(1), 11–12.

OFSTED (1998) *Inspection Report: Elliott Durham School, Nottingham*. Contract number: 930/5/700210. London: Office for Standards in Education.

Ortega, R. and Del Rey, R. (1999) The use of peer support in the SAVE project. Paper presented at the Ninth European Conference on Developmental Psychology, Island of Spetses, 1–5 September.

Österman, K., Björkqvist, K., Lagerspetz, K., Landau, S., Fraczek, A. and Pastorelli, C. (1997). Sex differences in styles of conflict resolution: a developmental and cross-cultural study with data from Finland, Israel, Italy and Poland. In D.P. Fry and K. Björkqvist (eds), *Cultural Variation in Conflict Resolution*, Mahwah, NJ: Lawrence Erlbaum.

Parkinson, A. (1999) *Accounting for Managers: Unit 4, Balancing the Budget*. Milton Keynes: Open University Press.

Polan, A. (1989) School: the inevitable democracy? In C. Harber and R. Meighan (eds), *The Democratic School: Education Management and the Practice of Democracy*. Ticknall: Education Now Publishing Cooperative.

Powell, S.D. and Makin, M. (1994) Enabling pupils with learning difficulties to reflect on their own thinking. *British Educational Research Journal*, 20(5), 579–93.

Rigby, K. and Slee, P. (1991) Bullying among Australian schoolchildren: reported behaviour and attitudes to victims. *Journal of Social Psychology*, 13, 615–27.

Roberts, M. (1994) *Skills for Self-managed Learning: Autonomous learning by research projects*. Ticknall: Education Now Publishing Cooperative.

Rogers, B. (1996) Mediation has certainly worked for us. *Education and Health*, 14(1), 1–4.

Rogers, C.R. (1951) *Client-centred Therapy*. Boston: Houghton Mifflin.

Rogers, K., Scherer-Thompson, J. and Laws, S. (1999) *Research Report on the Peer Support Programme*. London: Mental Health Foundation.

Ross, D.M. (1996) *Childhood Bullying and Teasing*. Alexandria, VA: American Counselling Association.

Salmivalli, C. (1999). Participant role approach to school bullying: implications for interventions. *Journal of Adolescence*, 22(4), 453–9.

Salmivalli, C., Lagerspetz, K., Björkqvist, K., Österman, K. and Kaukiainen, A. (1996) Bullying as a group process: participant roles and their relations to social status within the group. *Aggressive Behavior*, 22, 1–15.

Salmivalli, C., Kaukiainen, A., Kaistaniemi, L. and Lagerspetz, K. (1999) Self-evaluated self-esteem, peer-evaluated self-esteem and defensive egotism as predictors of adolescents' behaviour in bullying situations. *Personality and Social Psychology Bulletin*, 25, 1268–78.

Sandole, D.J.D. and Sandole, I.S. (eds), (1987) *Conflict Management and Problem Solving: Interpersonal to International Applications*. London: Frances Pinter.

Sarris, R. (1995) Resident staff as peer mentors. In S. Hatcher (ed.), *Peer Programs on the College Campus*. San Jose, CA: Resource Publications Inc.

Sartre, J.-P. (1948) *Existentialism and Humanism*. London: Eyre Methuen.

Save the Children/West Yorkshire Probation Service (1993) *Victim Offender Mediation Handbook*. Leeds: Leeds Mediation Service.

Severson, M. and Bankston, T. (1995) Social work and the pursuit of justice through mediation. *Social Work*, 40, 683–91.

Sharp, S. (1999) *Bullying Behaviour in Schools*. London: NFER.

Sharp, S. and Cowie, H. (1998) *Understanding and Supporting Children in Distress*. London: Sage.

Smith, P.K. and Sharp, S. (eds) (1994) *School Bullying: Insights and Perspectives*. London: Routledge.

Smith, P.K. and Shu, S. (2000) What good schools can do about bullying. *Childhood*, 7(2), 193–212.

Stacey, H. (1996a) Mediation into schools does go: an outline of the mediation process and how it can be used to promote positive relationships and effective conflict resolutions in schools. *Journal for Pastoral Education and Personal and Social Education*, 14(2), 7–10.

Stacey, H. (1996b) Peer mediation: skills training for life. *Primary Practice: The Journal of the National Primary Centre*, 3, 1–3.

Stacey, H. and Robinson, P. (1997) *Let's Mediate: A Teacher's Guide to Peer Support and Conflict Resolution Skills for All Ages*. Bristol: Lucky Duck Publishing.

Stacey, H., Robinson, P. and Cremin, D. (1997) Using conflict resolution and peer mediation to tackle bullying. In D.P. Tattum and G. Herbert (eds), *Bullying: Home, School and Community*. London: David Fulton Publishers.

Stuart, L.A. (1991) *Conflict Resolution Using Mediation Skills in the Elementary Schools*. A Report available from the Conflict Manager Program, Virginia, United States.

Sutton, J. and Smith, P.K. (1999) Bullying as a group process: an adaptation of the participant role approach. *Aggressive Behavior*, 25, 97–111.

Taylor, G. (1996) Creating a Circle of Friends: a case study. In H. Cowie and S. Sharp (eds), *Peer Counselling in Schools: a Time to Listen*. London: David Fulton Publishers.

Thompson, S. (1996) Peer mediation – a peaceful solution. *School-Counselor*, 44(2), 151–4.

Tinker, R. (1998) ABC: Peer counselling at Elliott Durham School. *Peer Support Networker*, 8(8): 8.

Topping, K. (1988) *The Peer Tutoring Handbook: Promoting Co-operative Learning*. Cambridge, MA: Brookline Books.

Topping, K. (1996) Reaching where adults cannot: peer education and peer counselling. *Educational Psychology in Practice*, 11(4), 23–9.

Topping, K. (1998) Paired learning in literacy. In K. Topping and S. Ehly (eds), *Peer-assisted Learning*. Mahwah, NJ: Lawrence Erlbaum.

Topping, K. and Ehly, S. (eds), (1998) *Peer-assisted Learning*. Mahwah, NJ: Lawrence Erlbaum.

Tyrrell, J. and Farrell, S. (1995) *Peer Mediation in Primary Schools*. University of Ulster, Northern Ireland.

Waterhouse, P. (1983) *Supported Self-study in Secondary Education*. London: CET.

Webb, A. and Kaye, P. (1996) 'A little help from my friends': a secondary school peer support programme. *Pastoral Care in Education*, 14(2), 21–5.

Weil, S.W. and McGill, I. (1989) *Making Sense of Experiential Learning: Diversity in Theory and Practice*. Milton Keynes: Society for Research in Higher Education/ Open University Press.

White, M. (1991) *Self-esteem: Promoting Positive Practices for Responsible Behaviour, Circle Time Strategies for Schools*. Cambridge: Daniels Publishing.

White, P. (1989) Educating courageous citizens. In C. Harber and R. Meighan (eds), *The Democratic School: Education Management and the Practice of Democracy*. Ticknall: Education Now Publishing Cooperative.

Whitney, I. and Smith, P.K. (1993) A survey on the nature and extent of bully/victim problems in junior/middle and secondary schools. *Educational Research*, 35, 3–25.

Zielasko, J., Paulson, P., Nwankwo, R., Stewart, G. and Hoppe, K. (1995) Peer education at university health services. In S. Hatcher (ed.), *Peer Programs on the College Campus*. San Jose, CA: Resource Publications Inc.

INDEX